SPOTLIGHT

COASTAL VIRGINIA

D1310969

MICHAELA RIVA GAASERUD

Contents

COASTAL VIRGINIA

COASTAL VIRGINIA

Coastal Virginia sounds like a simple concept: where the Atlantic Ocean meets the land. However, it's much more complicated than that. The Chesapeake Bay is a defining feature along the coast, and the area where it opens into the Atlantic Ocean has developed into one of the largest and busiest natural ports on the globe. Several large rivers empty into the Chesapeake Bay as well, including the Potomac, Rappahannock, James, and York Rivers.

The coastal region can be divided into five main areas. The first is the **Northern Neck,** which sits between the Potomac and Rappahannock Rivers, both of which flow into the bay. The Northern Neck is quiet and flat with many farms along the riverbanks. The area is quite historical and home to several noted sites including George Washington's birthplace. The second area is known as the **Historic Triangle,** which includes the colonial cities of Williamsburg, Jamestown, and Yorktown. These cities sit along the James and York Rivers, which also flow into the Chesapeake Bay. Next is the huge area of **Hampton Roads.** This is where everything converges. The rivers flow into the bay just to the north, and the Chesapeake Bay flows into the Atlantic Ocean just to the east. The main cities in this area are Newport News, Hampton, and Norfolk. Then we have Virginia Beach. The **Virginia Beach** resort area is truly on the Atlantic Coast. Our final region, **Virginia's Eastern Shore,** is sandwiched between the Chesapeake Bay on the west and the Atlantic Ocean on the east. It is sparsely populated compared to its mainland

HIGHLIGHTS

© AVALON TRAVEL

LOOK FOR ◖ TO FIND RECOMMENDED SIGHTS, ACTIVITIES, DINING, AND LODGING.

◖ **Colonial Williamsburg:** A living museum unmatched nationwide, Colonial Williamsburg takes visitors back in time. It's one of America's most popular family destinations (page 14).

◖ **Jamestown National Historic Site:** The original site of the Jamestown settlement spans centuries of history. Founded in 1607, it was an important settlement in the New World (page 25).

◖ **NAUTICUS National Maritime Center:** This nautical-themed science and technology center in Norfolk is also home to the 887-foot USS *Wisconsin* (page 44).

◖ **Virginia Beach Boardwalk:** The most popular beach resort in the state offers enough activity to keep visitors busy for days—plus wonderful access to miles of sand and surf (page 51).

◖ **Virginia Aquarium & Marine Science Center:** Hundreds of exhibits, live animals, and hands-on learning make this amazing aquarium one of the most popular attractions in the state (page 51).

◖ **Tangier Island:** This remote island in the middle of the Chesapeake Bay feels like another country. They even have their own language (page 64).

◖ **Chincoteague National Wildlife Refuge:** These 14,000 acres of wildlife refuge protect thousands of birds and a herd of wild ponies. Visitors can enjoy miles of natural beaches and hike and bike through the marsh (page 68).

neighbors and offers charming historical towns and ample bird-watching and fishing.

PLANNING YOUR TIME

Visiting Coastal Virginia requires some planning, a love of water, and no fear of bridges. Although there is some public transportation between specific cities, the easiest way to get around is by car. Highway 64 runs from Richmond down to the Historic Triangle and Hampton Roads areas, while Routes 17 and 3

traverse the Northern Neck. Route 13 runs the length of the Eastern Shore.

Coastal Virginia is a beautiful region but one that takes days, not hours to explore. If you are limited on time, select one or two key destinations such as Williamsburg and Virginia Beach, or maybe spend a day or two on the Eastern Shore. Wherever you decide to go, keep in mind that the area is heavily visited in the summer months, so you will likely have a few thousand close friends to share the experience

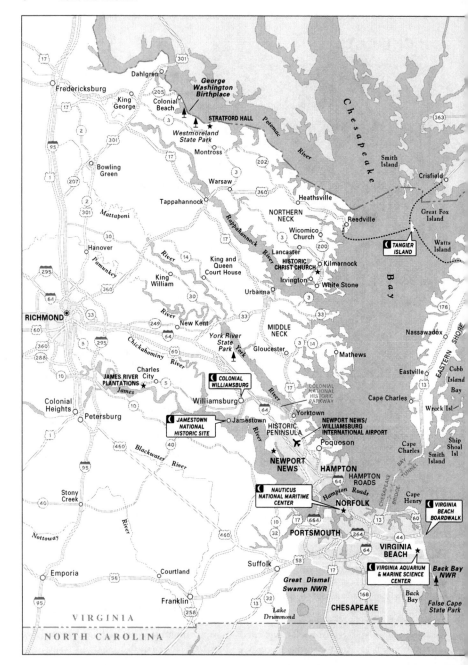

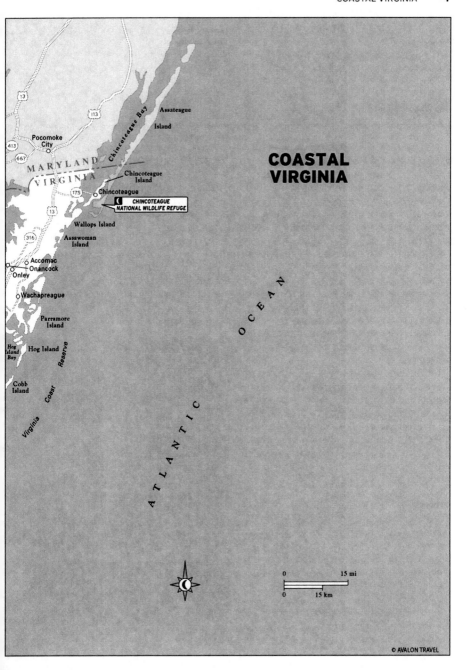

COASTAL
VIRGINIA

Assateague
Island

Chincoteague Bay

Pocomoke
City

13

113

413

66?

MARYLAND
VIRGINIA

Chincoteague
Island

175 Chincoteague

CHINCOTEAGUE
NATIONAL WILDLIFE REFUGE

13

Wallops Island

316

Assawoman
Island

Accomac
Onancock
Onley

Wachapreague

Parramore
Island

Hog
Island
Bay

Hog Island

Reserve

Cobb
Island

Coast

Virginia

ATLANTIC   OCEAN

0   15 mi

0   15 km

© AVALON TRAVEL

with, especially in the historical towns and beachfront areas.

If you are looking for a one-of-a-kind experience, spend a day visiting Tangier Island. This isolated sandbar of a town is 12 miles out in the Chesapeake Bay and almost feels like a completely different country.

Northern Neck

The Northern Neck is a peninsula bordered by the Potomac and Rappahannock Rivers, not far from the Chesapeake Bay in an area approximately 75 miles from Washington DC. The Northern Neck is laden with history and was explored as early as 1608 by the famed Captain John Smith. George Washington, who was born here, called the region the "Garden of Virginia" for the tidewater landscape and many forests and creeks that shape this area of the state.

During the steamboat era between 1813 and 1937, the Northern Neck supported a network of approximately 600 steamboats. These mechanical works of art were used to transport both people and goods throughout the Chesapeake Bay area.

In modern times, the Northern Neck is still rural and supports generations of a thriving fishing industry. It is also a popular area for recreational boating and water sports. It offers small-town charm, historical sites, colonial architecture, and marinas. Many establishments are only open seasonally, so if you are traveling during the colder months, a quick call ahead could pay off.

SIGHTS
George Washington Birthplace
Although the father of our country only lived in the Northern Neck until he was three years old, his birthplace on **Pope's Creek Plantation** (1732 Popes Creek Rd., Colonial Beach, 804/224-1732, ext. 227, www.nps.gov/gewa, daily 9am-5pm, free) is a lovely place to visit on the banks of the Potomac River. The National Park Service provides a visitor center with a film, exhibits, and bookstore. The actual house Washington was born in no longer exists (it burned down in 1779), but ranger talks about the historic area are offered on the hour between 10am and 4pm. There is a reconstructed colonial farm on-site with animals and tobacco operated by costumed interpreters. A one-mile nature trail is available and can be accessed from the picnic area. There is also a beach along the river, but no swimming is permitted. Relatives spanning five generations of Washington's family are buried on the site in the Washington Family Burial Ground, including George's father, grandfather, and great-grandfather.

© MICHAELA RIVA GAASERUD

George Washington birthplace

MICHAELA RIVA GAASERUD

Stratford Hall, birthplace of Robert E. Lee

Stratford Hall

Stratford Hall (483 Great House Rd., Stratford, 804/493-8038, www.stratfordhall. org, daily 9:30am-4pm, $10) is the birthplace of General Robert E. Lee. The beautiful brick mansion, which sits on 1,900 acres next to the Potomac River, was built in the late 1730s. It is furnished with 18th-century American and English pieces (including Lee's crib). The home has 16 fireplaces. Visitors can take a 45-minute house tour on the hour, walk six nature trails, enjoy the beach overlook, examine exhibits in a visitor center, and browse a gift shop. The dining room on-site can be reserved for groups of 15 or more for a special buffet.

Reedville

Reedville is a little gem of a town founded in 1867 and one jumping-off point to **Tangier Island** in the Chesapeake Bay. It is known for its thriving Atlantic menhaden fishing industry (menhaden are small, oily fish found in the mid-Atlantic) and was at one time the wealthiest city per capita in the country in the early 20th century. (Millionaire's Row, a string of Victorian mansions along the water attests to this affluence.) Reedville remains a major commercial fishing port, second behind Kodiak, Alaska.

Don't miss the **Reedville Fishermen's Museum** (504 Main St., 804/453-6529, www. rfmuseum.org, daily 10:30am-4:30pm, closed Dec. 19-25, Jan. 1-14, $5) on Cockrell's Creek. There are several parts to the museum: the **William Walker House,** a restored home built in 1875 that represents a watermen's home; the **Covington Building,** which houses temporary exhibits and a permanent collection; and the **Pendleton Building,** which contains a boat-building and model shop. In addition, there are two historic boats at the museum, a skipjack and deck boat. Both are on the National Register of Historic Places.

Irvington

The historic village of **Irvington** (www.irvingtonva.org) was established in 1891 during the steamboat era. A busy port on the well-traveled

Norfolk-Baltimore route, the town thrived during the early 1900s. The Great Fire of Irvington destroyed many businesses in June of 1917, coinciding with the decline of the steamboat era. In 1947, the town was put back on the map with the opening of the **Tides Inn Resort,** and today Irvington is a hip little town with boutique shopping, friendly dining, and several key attractions. It's easy to feel the fun vibe in Irvington. Just a stroll down Irvington Road will likely engage you in reading some fun sayings that are posted on signs in the gardens of shops and restaurants. Keep in mind that many establishments are closed on Monday.

The **Steamboat Era Museum** (156 King Carter Dr., 804/438-6888, www.steamboateramuseum.org, Thurs.-Sat. 10am-4pm, Sun. 1pm-4pm, by appointment only in winter, free, donations appreciated) is a delightful little museum in Irvington that preserves artifacts and information from the steamboat era of the Chesapeake Bay (1813-1937). Steamboats were a vital mode of transportation along the bay for both goods and people and the lifeline of the economy connecting the region to cities such as Norfolk, Virginia, and Baltimore, Maryland. This is the only museum fully dedicated to the steamboats of the Chesapeake Bay, and the docents are very entertaining and knowledgeable.

The most treasured historic structure in the Northern Neck is arguably the **Historic Christ Church** (420 Christ Church Rd., Weems, 804/438-6855, www.christchurch1735.org, year-round Mon.-Fri. 8:30am-4:30pm, Apr.-Nov. Sat. 10am-4pm, Sun. 2pm-5pm, weekends by appointment the rest of the year, $5). Less than two miles north of Irvington, the church was finished in 1735 and remains one of the few unaltered colonial churches in the United States. It was a center of social and political activity during colonial times, and Sunday service was a big event. In addition to being a place or worship, it was a place to exchange news and the cornerstone of the community. The detailed brickwork in the tall walls and a vaulted ceiling help make it one of the best-crafted Anglican parish churches of its time. Services are still held there, and the interior boasts a triple-decker pulpit, walnut altar, and high-backed pews. There is a reception center, **The Carter Reception Center** onsite that houses a museum covering the church and its founder Robert Carter. Guided tours are available from the center, and there is also a gift shop.

ENTERTAINMENT AND EVENTS

Many of the events in the Northern Neck revolve around water and nature. The **Blessing of the Fleet** is an annual event in Reedville that opens the fishing season on the first weekend of May. There is a parade of boats and the official blessing service. The **Reedville Bluefish Derby** is a large fishing tournament held annually in mid-June that features substantial cash prizes.

Mid-September brings the **Reedville Antique and Classic Boat Show** (www.acbs. org) featuring an antique boat parade. And mid-November is the time for the much anticipated **Reedville Fishermen's Museum Oyster Roast** (www.rfmuseum.org). Tickets go on sale in October and sell out quickly for this mouthwatering event.

Wine enthusiasts will enjoy the **Kilmarnock Wine Festival** (www.northernneckwinefestival. com) held annually at the end of June. It offers tastings and sales from local wineries along the **Chesapeake Bay Wine Trail** (www.chesapeakebaywinetrail.com), including more than a dozen wineries in Virginia in the Chesapeake Bay area that can be visited year-round. Each offers wine tastings, sales, gift shops, and tours.

SPORTS AND RECREATION
Westmoreland State Park
Westmoreland State Park (1650 State Park Rd., Montross, 804/493-8821, www.dcr. virginia.gov, open 24 hours, $4) along the Potomac River offers riverfront beaches, hiking trails, a public pool, kayak and paddleboat rentals, a pond, and cliffs housing fossils. It became one of Virginia's first state parks in 1936. This 1,300-acre park also provides camping cabins for rent year-round and 133 seasonal campsites. The Potomac River Retreat is a lodge that is

THE STEAMBOAT ERA

Steamboat Era Museum in Irvington

Steamboats came on the scene in the Chesapeake Bay in the early 1800s. As their popularity rose, they quickly became as important to the cities along the bay as the railroad was to the rest of the country. By the mid-1800s, steamboats were used to transport everything including passengers, mail, and goods.

By the turn of the 20th century, nearly 600 steamboats cruised the bay, carrying thousands of passengers to the key cities of Norfolk, Virginia, and Baltimore, Maryland, and every place in between. Steamboat excursions became extremely popular, and commerce flourished. Farms grew as their potential for distributing goods expanded, and many canneries were built near the shore. At one time, 85 percent of the world's oyster trade came from the Chesapeake Bay, and these little delicacies were shipped via steamboat.

The 20th century brought the development of the automobile and the slow demise of the steamboat. As cars became affordable and more common, passenger traffic on the steamboats began to dwindle. Still, the boats were used for commerce until the 1930s, when a hurricane in 1933 wiped out many of the Chesapeake Bay wharfs.

The final excursion of a popular steamboat named the *Anne Arundel* was made on September 14, 1937. That day is still celebrated in Virginia as "Steamboat Era Day."

Additional information on the steamboat era can be found on the Steamboat Era Museum website, www.steamboateramuseum.org.

also available for rent in the park and holds 15 overnight guests and up to 40 people for meetings. There is a small camp store, but it's best to bring your own food as they have limited drinks and snacks. Dogs and cats are allowed in the park and cabins for an additional overnight fee. Take in the great view of the Potomac from **Horsehead Cliffs,** and don't miss a stroll down fossil beach where you might even find some ancient shark's teeth. There is a visitor center on-site that is open daily 8am-4:30pm.

Westmoreland Berry Farm

If picking berries makes you feel connected to colonial times, stop by the **Westmoreland Berry Farm** (1235 Berry Farm Ln., Colonial Beach, 804/224-9171, www.westmorelandberryfarm.com, May-Nov. Mon.-Sat. 9am-5pm, Sun. 10am-5pm). This riverside farm (on the Rappahannock River) offers visitors the opportunity to pick their own fruit and berries (depending on what's in season). Or you can browse their country store for fresh produce, visit their farm, or lunch at the country kitchen.

Canoeing and Kayaking

The nation's first national water trail, the **Captain John Smith Chesapeake National Historic Trail** (www.smithtrail.net) includes 3,000 miles of routes through the Chesapeake Bay, Northern Neck, Middle Neck, and their tributaries in Virginia and Maryland. The route was inspired by the regions explored in the 17th century by Captain John Smith.

Two-hour interpretive kayak trips are offered at **Westmoreland State Park** (800/933-7275, $19 solo kayak, $25 tandem) and include basic instruction and a guided trip along the shoreline.

Fishing

Captain Billy's Charters (545 Harveys Neck Rd., Heathsville, www.captbillyscharters. com, $650-700 for six people for fishing, $15-25 per person for cruises) runs boat charters for both fishing and cruising from the **Ingram Bay Marina** into the Chesapeake Bay. **Crabbe Charter Fishing** (51 Railway Dr., Heathsville,

www.crabbescharterfishing.com, $600 for up to six people) is another charter fishing company in the Northern Neck. They offer outings year-round.

Bird-Watching

Bird-watchers have many opportunities to view songbirds, waterfowl, eagles, and wading birds along the **Northern Neck Loop** birding trail (www.dgif.virginia.gov). This driving trail passes by historical sites and through an area known to have the largest population of bald eagles on the Eastern Seaboard.

ACCOMMODATIONS
$100-200

Ma Margaret's House (249 Greenfield Rd., Reedville, 804/453-9110, www.mamargaretshouse.com, $125-175) is a cozy, recently renovated 4,000 square foot home built in 1914 that belonged to the owner's grandparents. It offers several guest suites, a lot of privacy, and a wonderful staff.

$200-300

◖ **The Hope and Glory Inn** (65 Tavern Rd., Irvington, 800/497-8228, www.hopeandglory. com, $200-400) is a boutique inn with 6 rooms and 10 cottages. Lavish and romantic, with a little sense of humor, the inn was originally a schoolhouse built in 1890. The school had two front doors, one for girls and one for boys. It now boasts beautifully appointed rooms, lush gardens, and even a moon garden with flowers that only bloom in the evening. There's a spa, meeting facilities, and a dock for boating, kayaking, or canoeing on-site as well as an outdoor pool and an outdoor bath (that is not a typo, there really is a claw-foot tub in an enclosed area outside). Tennis and three golf courses are a short distance away. The town of Irvington, which sits on the Chesapeake Bay, offers trendy shopping and a fun atmosphere.

Wine lovers won't want to miss visiting **The Dog and Oyster,** the Hope and Glory Inn's vineyard, named for the establishment's rescue dogs who guard their grapes from area wildlife and also in honor of the local oysters which pair

The Hope and Glory Inn in Irvington

well with their wines. If the weather is nice, enjoy a bottle of wine on the porch.

The **Tides Inn** (480 King Carter Dr., Irvington, 804/438-5000, www.tidesinn.com, $190-375) is a well-known resort bordered by the Potomac and Rappahannock Rivers and the Chesapeake Bay. This romantic waterfront inn hangs on the banks of Carters Creek as a little oasis of red-roofed buildings offering peace and relaxation to visitors of all ages. It features luxurious waterfront accommodations, golf, a marina, and a spa. There is also a sailing school with many options for lessons and family sailing activities. Packages include some geared toward golf, family vacations, and romance. There are also several good restaurants on-site and the inn is dog-friendly.

CAMPING

Westmoreland State Park (1650 State Park Rd., Montross, 804/493-8821, www.dcr.virginia.gov, open 24 hours) offers 133 campsites and a handful of camping cabins. Camping sites feature a fire ring grill or box grills.

Forty-two sites offer electric and water hookups for $27 per night, sites without these amenities are $20 per night. There is also one group tent site that can accommodate up to 40 people ($122). Camping cabins have a maximum capacity of four and require a two-night minimum stay. Cabins do not have bathrooms, kitchens, heat, air-conditioning, or linens. Bathhouses are available on-site for all campers.

FOOD
Reedville

The Crazy Crab Restaurant (902 Main St., 804/453-6789, www.reedvillemarina.com, $14-24), at the Reedville Marina, is a casual seafood restaurant offering an abundance of local seafood choices and a few land-based choices. The waterfront view from the restaurant is nice, the atmosphere is fun, and outdoor seating is available. Hours vary greatly each season.

Cockrell's Seafood (567 Seaboard Dr., 804/453-6326, www.smithpointseafood.com, Wed.-Sat. 11am-3pm, $7-15) is a seafood deli on the waterfront. The atmosphere is very casual with picnic tables, and they serve delicious crab dishes.

Satisfy your sweet tooth at **Chitterchats Ice Cream** (846 Main St., 804/453-3335, $5-10). This family-oriented ice cream shop offers delicious homemade ice cream with around 20 flavors.

Irvington

Nate's Trick Dog Café (4357 Irvington Rd., 804/438-6363, www.trickdogcafe.com, Tues.-Sat. 5pm-close, $20-33) is a trendy little find in a town full of fun surprises. A statue of the "Trick Dog" guards the entrance and brings good luck to those who pet it. The statue, which depicts a terrier, was found in the basement of the local Opera House after a devastating fire in 1917 that destroyed many local businesses. The statue was sooty and dirty, and was called the Trick Dog since it didn't need food or water. It is an institution at this fine little restaurant and, judging by the good times and laughter flowing out of its doors, seems to be working its magic. The menu offers tasty entrées such as jumbo crab cakes, filet of yellowfin tuna, and shrimp and grits. There's also a bar menu of interesting finger food, burgers, and sandwiches. This place is worth a stop.

◖ **The Local** (4337 Irvington Rd., 804/438-9356, daily 7:30am-3pm, under $10) is a good choice for a grabbing a sandwich at lunchtime. This friendly little restaurant offers a cute decor and a good selection of sandwiches and salads, including a unique menu of panini and wraps. A personal recommendation is the "Tom" wrap, which has turkey, brie, apples, and honey mustard. It goes well with a Northern Neck soda. They also serve ice cream, great coffee, and beer and wine.

INFORMATION AND SERVICES

For additional information on the Northern Neck, visit www.northernneck.org.

Williamsburg and the Historic Triangle

The "Historic Triangle," as it is known, consists of Williamsburg, Jamestown, and Yorktown. These three historic towns are just minutes apart and retain some of our country's most important Revolutionary War history.

WILLIAMSBURG

Williamsburg is one of America's earliest planned cities. It was designed as the capital of the Virginia Colony, which was the most populous of the British colonies in America in 1699. As such, Williamsburg had the oldest legislative assembly in the New World, and a series of elaborate capitol buildings were erected as the city developed into the thriving center of Virginia. The original capital, Jamestown, had been founded just five miles away in 1607. The governmental seat was moved by the Virginia Assembly to a site between the James and York Rivers known as Middle Plantation, but the name was changed to Williamsburg after King William III of England. Williamsburg remained the capital of Virginia until 1780, when it was moved to its current location in Richmond.

Today, when people speak of Williamsburg, they most often are referring to this capital area known now as **Colonial Williamsburg.** This original capital city is the prime destination for not only the preservation of American colonial history but also its interpretation. However, although Colonial Williamsburg is the best-known attraction in the Williamsburg area, there are many other attractions nearby including the historic **College of William & Mary** and a number of popular theme parks.

Sights
◖ **COLONIAL WILLIAMSBURG**
Colonial Williamsburg (757/229-1000, www.colonialwilliamsburg.com, one-day ticket, $39.95, three-day ticket, $47.50) is the largest

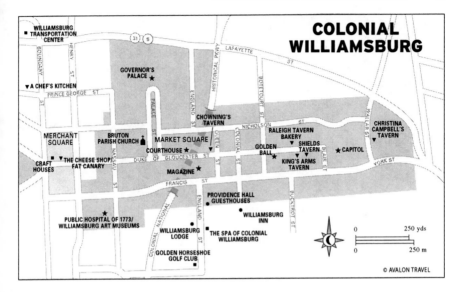

living museum in the country, and it is truly a historical marvel. It is open 365 days a year and run by the private, not-for-profit **Colonial Williamsburg Foundation.** The museum encompasses the restored 18th-century colonial Virginia capital city, which was the center of politics in Virginia for 80 years, featuring the real city streets and buildings that were erected during that time. There are historical exhibits, taverns, shops featuring original trades, and many other sites within the museum area. Ticketholders gain access to the historical buildings, theatrical performances, 15 site tours, 35 exhibitions, and museums. It is free to wander the streets themselves.

Although Colonial Williamsburg is open all year, if you are flexible in choosing when to visit, spring and fall can be the most rewarding. This is when crowds are less dense and the temperatures are the most moderate (plan to do a lot of walking around the city). Summer is the busiest tourist season since school is out of session, and it can also be very hot and humid, especially in August.

It is best to begin your visit at the **Colonial Williamsburg Regional Visitor Center** (101 Visitor Center Dr., 757/220-7645, daily 8:45am-5pm). The helpful staff can help you put together an itinerary for your stay that will allow you to hit the highlights and choose additional sites you are interested in. You can also purchase Colonial Williamsburg tickets and learn about events and activities taking place during your time here. The highlights in Colonial Williamsburg can be seen over a weekend, but to really soak in the atmosphere, it can be fun to spend an extra day or two, or to make it your base for exploring other nearby attractions.

Everything within the museum area is neat, clean, well-maintained, and historically correct. The staff is dressed in period clothing and plays roles very seriously. Conversations between staff members and the public are always in character. Visitors become "Residents of the City" and are submerged in history in this unique Revolutionary era and can enjoy authentic era dining and shopping while staying in hotels with all modern conveniences.

There's a large pedestrian area through the center of the historical enclave along **Duke of Gloucester Street.** Horses and horse-drawn carriages are allowed on the street if they are part of the museum. President Franklin D.

Colonial Williamsburg is the largest living museum in the country.

© MICHAELA RIVA GAASERUD

Roosevelt called Duke of Gloucester Street the "most historic avenue in all of America."

Market Square, the center of activity in Colonial Williamsburg, straddles Duke of Gloucester Street. Residents went there on a regular basis (if not daily) to purchase goods and socialize. Visitors can experience the same atmosphere along Duke of Gloucester Street, where the official Williamsburg brand shops are located.

Ticket-holding visitors can explore a variety of historical buildings such as the reconstructed **Capitol,** that sits at the east end of Duke of Gloucester Street (daily 9am-5pm). The current building is the third capitol to stand on the site, but it is very much the same as the original completed in 1705. A trip through this tall brick building is like a history lesson on the government in colonial Virginia and the contributions the colony made to the American Revolution. Evening programs in the Capitol include reenactments of political and social events that actually occurred here in the 18th century. One day a year, a naturalization

ceremony is carried out at the Capitol for immigrants becoming Americans, to carry on a tradition that began nearly 300 years ago.

The impressive **Governors Palace,** built between 1706 and 1722 at the end of Palace Green Street off of West Duke of Gloucester Street, was home to seven royal governors, Thomas Jefferson, and Patrick Henry. After many decades as a symbol of the power of royal England, the home served as a military headquarters and twice as a wartime hospital (156 soldiers and 2 women are buried in the garden as a result of the Battle of Yorktown). The original structure burned to the ground in 1781, but the building was reconstructed to its current grandeur in the 1930s. Since then, the home has been furnished with American and British antiques in the Colonial Revival style. This is perhaps the most popular site in Colonial Williamsburg, so make it first on your list, early in the day, before the crowds set in.

The **Courthouse** (Duke of Gloucester Street) is a focal point of Market Square and one that no doubt put fear in the hearts of many criminals in its day as the local government seat. It was built in 1770 and is one of Williamsburg's original 18th-century buildings, continuing to be the location of municipal and county courts until 1932. The building's T-shaped design is common to many Virginia courthouses, but an octagonal cupola and several other formal design elements (such as a weather vane, arched windows, and a cantilevered pediment) make it distinct in appearance. The signing of the Treaty of Paris (ending the Revolutionary War) was announced at the Courthouse.

A small but fascinating building is the **Magazine** (Duke of Gloucester Street). This original building was constructed in 1715 at the request of Governor Alexander Spotswood, who wanted a solid brick house to store and protect weapons and ammunition. The Magazine is well known for its role in the **Gunpowder Incident** on April 20, 1775, a conflict which occurred early in the Revolutionary War between the royal governor, Lord Dunmore, and the militia (led by Patrick Henry). Lord Dunmore gave orders to remove all the gunpowder from the Magazine and move it to a Royal Navy ship. This led to unrest in Virginia and the movement of Patrick Henry's militia toward Williamsburg to return the gunpowder to the colony. The incident was resolved peacefully, but Dunmore retreated to a naval ship, thus ending royal governing of the colony. The incident helped move Virginia toward revolution.

Many craftspeople, some who have spent years learning the trade, create colonial-era crafts in dozens of shops throughout the living museum. Visitors can watch blacksmiths and armorers shape tools, weapons, and hardware out of iron and steel at **Anderson's Blacksmith Shop & Public Armoury** (E. Duke of Gloucester Street, daily 9am-5pm) or visit the **Wigmaker** (E. Duke of Gloucester Street, Sun., Mon., Wed., Thurs., and Fri. 9am-5pm) to learn the importance of the 18th-century wigmaker and barber and how this trade was essential to the social structure of the day. Other crafters include the **Shoemaker** (W.

the Magazine in Colonial Williamsburg

© MICHAELA RIVA GAASERUD

Duke of Gloucester Street, Sun., Tues., Wed., Thurs., Fri., and Sat. 9am-5pm), the **Weaver** (W. Duke of Gloucester Street, Sun., Thurs., Fri., and Sat. 9am-5pm) and the **Bindery** (E. Duke of Gloucester Street, daily 1pm-5pm).

A number of historic taverns and restaurants are also located in Colonial Williamsburg and serve authentic colonial-style food. Look for the colonial flags out in front of the buildings. If a flag is out, it means the establishment is open.

More than 20 tours, both guided and self-led, are included in a Colonial Williamsburg admission ticket. The visitor center is the best place to find out what tours are offered on the day(s) you are there and what time they leave. Some popular tours include the **Freshest Advices for Travelers, Archaeology Walking Tours,** and the **Tavern Ghost Walk.** Dates and times change daily.

WILLIAMSBURG ART MUSEUMS

Two top-notch art museums, the **DeWitt Wallace Decorative Arts Museum** (757/220-7554, daily 10am-7pm) and the **Abby Aldrich Rockefeller Folk Art Museum** (757/220-7554, daily 10am-7pm) are located in the same building and can be reached by walking through the **Public Hospital of 1773** (326 W. Francis St., admission is included with the Colonial Williamsburg ticket). The DeWitt Wallace Decorative Arts Museum opened in 1985, funded by a generous donation from DeWitt and Lila Wallace, the founders of *Readers Digest*. It houses a large collection of American and British art and antiques, including the world's most extensive collection of southern furniture. The Abby Aldrich Rockefeller Folk Art Museum features a colorful variety of paintings, sculptures, and other art forms that are hung on the walls and ceilings. Each was created by self-taught artists and shows an imaginative array of details and color selections. There is also a kid-friendly animal-themed exhibit called Down on the Farm. While you're there, take in the exhibits at the Public Hospital. It was the first facility in North America dedicated to caring for the mentally ill. In this day and age, the hospital is

seen as part jail, part infirmary, and the treatments used in the 18th and 19th centuries are thankfully just part of history.

THE COLLEGE OF WILLIAM & MARY

Early on, Williamsburg developed into a hub for learning. **The College of William & Mary** (102 Richmond Rd., www.wm.edu), which is the second oldest college in the country, was founded in 1693. It is just west of Colonial Williamsburg and an easy walk from the colonial city. William & Mary turned out many famous early political leaders including Thomas Jefferson, John Tyler, and James Monroe. Today, the 1,200-acre campus is bustling with students. Visitors can enjoy a handful of historical attractions right on campus, including the **Sir Christopher Wren Building,** which was built 1695 and is known for being the oldest college building in the country. It was named for a royal architect, Christopher Wren, although concrete evidence has not been found that he actually designed it.

WILLIAMSBURG WINERY

Wine lovers will want to stop in for a tour and tasting at the **Williamsburg Winery** (5800 Wessex Hundred, 757/258-0899, www.williamsburgwinery.com, Mar. 16-Oct. 31 Mon.-Sat. 10am-6pm, Sun. 11am-6pm, Nov. 1-Mar. 15 Mon.-Sat. 10am-5pm, Sun. 11am-5pm, $10), about a 10-minute drive from the Colonial Williamsburg visitor center. The winery is Virginia's largest and accounts for one-quarter of all the wine produced in the state. Tours are available daily on the half hour.

BUSCH GARDENS WILLIAMSBURG

Busch Gardens Williamsburg (1 Busch Gardens Blvd., 800/343-7946, www.seaworldparks.com, mid-May-Labor Day Mon.-Thurs. 10am-6pm, Fri. 10am-8pm, Sat. 10am-10pm, Sun. 10am-9pm, reduced schedule the rest of the year, $67) is a theme park with rides, European villages, shows, exhibits, and exclusive tours. The park is less than five miles southeast of Williamsburg and is owned by SeaWorld. Hair-raising roller coasters, water rides, authentic food, and special attractions for little kids are just part of the fun at this beautiful park. Test your nerves on the Griffon, a 205-foot dive coaster (the tallest in the world), where brave riders free-fall at 75 miles per hour. Thrill seekers will also enjoy the Verbolten, one of the park's newest editions, an indoor/outdoor multi-launch coaster set in Germany's Black Forest. This coaster winds through the dark and ends with a heart-pounding plunge toward the Rhine River. Busch Gardens is also home of the classic Loch Ness Monster: a popular 13-story, double loop roller coaster that made the park famous nearly 30 years ago. This popular park also offers an Oktoberfest Village, a high-tech simulator that takes passengers over Europe, and animal attractions such as Jack Hanna's Wild Reserve, where visitors can see and learn about endangered and exotic animals.

WATER COUNTRY USA
Busch Gardens Williamsburg's sister park, **Water Country USA** (176 Water Country Pkwy., 800/343-7946, www.watercountry-usa.com, Memorial Day-Labor Day daily 10am-close, $48) is the largest water theme park in the mid-Atlantic. It is approximately three miles southeast of Williamsburg, just north of Busch Gardens. The park offers waterslides, pools, and more than 30 rides for kids of all ages as well as restaurants and live entertainment.

Entertainment and Events
Colonial Williamsburg doesn't shut down after dark. A variety of tours are available, including **Ghosts of Williamsburg Tours** (345 W. Duke of Gloucester St., 877/624-4678, www.theghosttour.com, daily 8pm, $11), a candlelit walking ghost tour of the town, and authentic taverns offer a relaxing end to a day of sightseeing. The **Kimball Theatre** (4242 W. Duke of Gloucester St., 757/565-8588, www.colonial-williambsburg.com) is a film and stage venue right in the middle of Colonial Williamsburg in Merchants Square. It offers programming in alliance with the College of William & Mary,

including foreign, classic, and documentary films along with live concerts.

Outside of the historic center—but only minutes away—visitors can play pool and enjoy live music on some nights at the **Corner Pocket** (4805 Courthouse St., 757/220-0808, www.thecornerpocket.us, Mon.-Tues. 11:30am-1am, Wed.-Sat. 11:30am-2am, Sun. 3pm-1am), an upscale pool hall.

Many festivals are held throughout the year in Williamsburg. The **Colonial Williamsburg Early Music Festival** (Historic Area, www.earlymusic.org) is held for four days at the end of September and showcases musical instruments that were popular in colonial Virginia. The fifes and drums play daily in the historic area, but during the festival many other instruments are featured and lectures are held about their origins.

The **Virginia Celtic Gathering and Highland Games** (www.wsfonline.org) is an annual event held in the beginning of October featuring Celtic pageantry, pub gatherings, music, sing-alongs, and authentic athletic events such as the "clachneart" stone toss.

Busch Gardens Williamsburg hosts an annual **Howl-o-scream** (1 Busch Gardens Blvd., www.seaworldparks.com) event starting in mid-September and running all through October on the weekends. This horror fest is for brave souls of all ages and features scary shows, creepy creatures lurking about the park, and fun characters for the littlest goblins.

The holiday season is a very popular time to visit Colonial Williamsburg. The **Grand Illumination** in early December is an eagerly awaited street festival where the entire historic area is decorated with traditional natural adornments for the season such as pinecones, evergreen branches, and candles. The area flickers at night by candlelight as carols are sung, concerts are held, and fireworks light up the night. Holiday festivities continue until the **First Night** celebration on New Year's Eve.

Shopping
Williamsburg offers endless shops. Strip malls

and outlet stores can be found in much of the area surrounding Colonial Williamsburg. For unique souvenirs, try stopping in the **Craft Houses** (420 W. Duke of Gloucester St., 757/220-7747) run by the Colonial Williamsburg Foundation. Pewter and ceramic gifts, jewelry, and folk art are for sale in the traditional style. Other favorite shops in the historic district include **The Prentis Store** (214 E. Duke of Gloucester St., 757/229-1000), which sells handcrafted leather pieces, pottery, furniture, ironware, and baskets; the **Market House,** an open-air market on Duke of Gloucester Street that sells hats, toys, and other handmade items; and the **Golden Ball** (406 E. Duke of Gloucester St., 757/229-1000) that sells one-of-a-kind jewelry.

Sports and Recreation
GOLF
The **Golden Horseshoe Golf Club** (401 S. England St., 757/220-7696, www.colonial-williamsburg.com, $45-75) is part of Colonial Williamsburg and offers 45 walkable holes. This scenic course is well-maintained and has been given accolades in publications such as *GOLF Magazine* and *Golfweek Magazine.*

The **Kingsmill Resort** (1010 Kingsmill Rd., 757/253-1703. www.kingsmill.com, $60-149) offers three championship 18-hole courses that are open to the public (one of which was ranked in the top 10 for women by *Golf Digest*).

The award-winning **Williamsburg National Golf Club** (3700 Centerville Rd., 757/258-9642, www.wngc.com, $50-79) has two 18-hole courses.

SPAS
The **Spa of Colonial Williamsburg** (757/253-2277, www.colonialwilliamsburg.com) is behind the Williamsburg Inn on East Francis Street. Enjoy treatments from botanicals used by the early settlers or a variety of soaks and massages. Packages are available.

HORSEBACK RIDING
If somehow horseback riding seems appropriate while visiting Williamsburg, contact **Lakewood**

Trails (575/566-9633, www.stonehousestables. com, $65) for one-hour guided trail rides.

GO APE TREETOP ADVENTURE
For something completely different, try a **Go Ape** (5537 Centerville Rd., 888/520-7322, www.goape.com, $55) Treetop Adventure. This kid- and adult-oriented adventure course includes high wires, ladders, tunnels, zip lines, and a lot of treetop excitement.

Accommodations
If Colonial Williamsburg is the focus of your Williamsburg trip, and you'd like to be submerged in the Revolutionary city, book a room in one of the Colonial Williamsburg Foundation hotels or guesthouses. These are conveniently located near the living museum sites and have a historic feel to them. Reservations, especially during the peak summer months, should be made in advance.

COLONIAL WILLIAMSBURG FOUNDATION
The **Colonial Williamsburg Foundation** maintains five hotels/lodges and 26 guesthouses. Each offers a different atmosphere and price range. Hotel guests have access to a terrific fitness facility located behind the Williamsburg Inn that includes a spa, state-of-art fitness room, indoor lap pool, and two gorgeous outdoor pools. Hotel guests also receive the best rate on general admission passes and discounts on special events. Reservations are handled through the foundation (www.colonialwilliamsburg.com).

The **Colonial Houses** (757/253-2277, $150-475) are individual colonial homes and rooms, each with a unique history. The number of rooms per house varies, but all are decorated with authentic reproductions of period pieces such as canopy beds and all have modern amenities. Look out over Duke of Gloucester Street, or sleep in the home where Thomas Jefferson lived while attending The College of William & Mary. Some homes are original historical buildings and others are replicas.

The luxurious ◖ **Williamsburg Inn** (136

© MICHAELA RIVA GAASERUD

Williamsburg Inn, adjacent to Colonial Williamsburg

E. Francis St., 757/253-2277, $400-620) was built in 1937 by John D. Rockefeller Jr., and the decor and furnishings in the lobby are still arranged exactly the way Mrs. Rockefeller designed it. This stately, upscale hotel has hosted many heads of state including President Dwight D. Eisenhower, Queen Elizabeth II, and Sir Winston Churchill. In 1983, the inn welcomed the Economic Summit of Industrialized Nations, hosted by President Ronald Reagan. It is listed on the National Register of Historic Places, but offers modern first-class accommodations in its 62 guest rooms. The hotel was the first in the United States to have central air-conditioning. Each elegant and spacious room is appointed with furnishings likened to an English country estate. The setting and decor are charming, and the service is excellent. Mrs. Rockefeller wished for guests to feel at home in the inn and as such instilled a warmth throughout the staff that still radiates today. Every last detail is attended to in their luxurious rooms, from beautifully tiled temperature-controlled showers to a fresh white rose in the bathrooms (the rose is the official inn flower) and little comforts like vanity mirrors and nightlights. The hotel is centrally located adjacent to Colonial Williamsburg. The Golden Horseshoe Golf Club is located behind the inn, and daily participatory events such as lawn bowling are offered to guests. There are two restaurants on-site (one formal dining room and a more casual lounge), and the hotel is very family-friendly.

The **Williamsburg Lodge** (310 S. England St., 757/253-2277, $145-225) is decorated in the classic Virginia style. Colorful fabric, leather, and warm woods give this hotel a lodge feel. This 300-room hotel hosts many conferences, and its unique garden provides a relaxing focal point. The rooms are spacious, the lodge is conveniently located near historic Colonial Williamsburg, and it's an easy walk to the attractions.

The **Providence Hall Guesthouses** (305 S. England St., 757/253-2277, $275-305) is in a quiet area near the Williamsburg Inn. It offers 43 large, bright rooms in a quiet, parklike setting with a more modern look to it. The hotel is pet-friendly.

The **Williamsburg Woodlands Hotel and Suites** (105 Visitor Center Dr., 757/253-2277, $115-210) is next to the visitor center for Colonial Williamsburg. This 300-room hotel offers contemporary rooms in a wooded setting. It is one of the least expensive options of the Colonial Williamsburg Foundation hotels.

The **Governor's Inn** (506 N. Henry St., 757/253-2277, $70-100) is a short walk from historic Colonial Williamsburg and the visitor center. This 200-room hotel offers economy accommodations and a seasonal outdoor pool.

OUTSIDE COLONIAL WILLIAMSBURG

There are quite a few choices for accommodations outside Colonial Williamsburg. Many are within an easy drive to the historic area.

The **Marriott's Manor Club at Ford's Colony** (101 St. Andrews Dr., 757/258-1120, www.marriott.com, $129-305) is in the private community of Ford's Colony and offers colonial architecture, deluxe guest rooms, and one- and two-bedroom villas. Each villa has a kitchen, living/dining area, washers and dryers, a balcony or patio, and a fireplace. This is a great place for families or groups who need a bit more space or plan an extended stay. Colonial Williamsburg and the College of William & Mary are about a 15-minute drive away, and Busch Gardens is about 20 minutes. There's a spa and golf course in the community, a fitness center, indoor and outdoor pools, and a sport court. Rooms are nicely appointed, and the buildings are spread out on a well-manicured property.

The **Wedmore Place** (5810 Wessex Hundred, 757/941-0310, www.wedmoreplace. com, $195-575) offers 28 individually decorated rooms in a variety of price ranges. Each room is designed after a European province and a different time in history, including all the furnishing and wall hangings. The 300-acre farm is also the site of the Williamsburg Winery and is about a 10-minute drive to the Colonial Williamsburg visitor center.

If you're looking for a kid-oriented hotel,

the **Great Wolf Lodge** (549 E. Rochambeau Dr., 757/229-9700, www.greatwolf.com, $239-410) provides endless amusement for the little ones. This Northwoods-themed lodge offers 405 guest rooms and a huge indoor water park, complete with waterslides, a wave pool, and a tree house. It is a four-season resort.

The **Kingsmill Resort and Spa** (1010 Kingsmill Rd., 757/253-1703, www.kingsmill. com, $219-609) offers 425 luxurious rooms and suites (with up to three bedrooms) as well as breathtaking views of the James River. It also has golf, a spa, an indoor pool, and summer children's programs. This is a great place for a romantic getaway or to spend time with friends playing golf or taking a spa day.

Camping

There are several good options for camping in Williamsburg. The **Anvil Campground** (5243 Mooretown Rd., 800/633-4442, www. anvilcampground.com, $30-140) offers 77 campsites and two cottages. It has been in operation since 1954 and is close to the historic Williamsburg attractions with shuttle service available to attractions, restaurants, and shopping. The **Williamsburg KOA Campground** (4000 Newman Rd., 757/565-2734, www.williamsburgkoa.com, starting at $40) is another good option close to Colonial Williamsburg and the theme parks. They offer 180 acres of wooded sites and patio sites (with more than 100 sites total). They also offer bus service to attractions in the peak season. Two additional campgrounds in Williamsburg are the **Outdoor World of Williamsburg Campground** (4301 Rochambeau Dr., 757/566-3021, $56), with 149 sites, and the **American Heritage R.V. Park** (146 Maxton Ln., 757/566-2133, $54), with 103 sites.

Food
AMERICAN

If you just need to grab a quick sandwich or you'd like to enjoy a gourmet cheese platter and a glass of wine, stop in **The Cheese Shop** (410 Duke of Gloucester St., 757/220-0298, Mon.-Sat. 10am-6pm, Sun. 11am-6pm, under

$15) in Merchants Square. They make custom cheese plates (from 200 varieties of imported and domestic cheese) at their cheese counter (to the left) and deli sandwiches at the back of the store (try their chicken salad, it has just enough bacon to taste wonderful but not enough to feel guilty). The store also carries fresh baked bread and a variety of snacks and drinks. Their wine cellar has more than 4,000 bottles of wine. There's seating outside (pay before you exit).

The **❰ Fat Canary** (410 Duke of Gloucester St., 757/220-3333, www.fatcanarywilliamsburg.com, daily 5pm-10pm, $28-39) in Merchants Square is named for the wine brought to the New World by ships that stopped in the Canary Islands for supplies. The wine was called a "canary" and this wonderful restaurant knows their wine. Widely considered one of the top restaurants in Williamsburg, The Fat Canary is an upscale restaurant that delivers an interesting menu of mouthwatering entrées such as quail, scallops, lamb, and beef tenderloin. They also have delicious desserts. The restaurant has a romantic ambience with soft pendant lighting and friendly service. This is a great place for a date or to relax after a day touring Colonial Williamsburg. Reservations are strongly suggested.

For a truly unique dining experience, make reservations at **A Chef's Kitchen** (501 Prince George St., 757/564-8500, www.achefskitchen.biz, Tues.-Sat. 6:30pm, $85) in the heart of Williamsburg. This food destination allows guests to learn about the fare they are eating and how it's prepared while being entertained by a talented chef. The fixed price menu is for a multicourse meal in which recipes are prepared, served, and paired with great wines. Diners sit at elegant long tables in tiered rows. The menu changes monthly, but sample dishes include asparagus and sweet pea soup, scallion and lime Gulf shrimp cake, roast rack of lamb, and strawberries sabayon in lace cup cookie. This small restaurant only seats 26 people, and it only offers one seating per night, so reservations are a must. Plan for 2-3 hours of dining time.

EUROPEAN

What do you get when you cross an art gallery with delicious, beautifully prepared food? The answer is **Artcafe26** (5107-2 Center St., 757/565-7788, www.artcafe26.com, Tues.-Thurs. 10:30am-5pm, Fri. 10:30am-9:30pm, Sat. 8:30am-3pm, 6pm-9:30pm, Sun. 10am-2pm, $35-39, tasting menu available) in the New Town area of Williamsburg. The dinner tasting menu is exceptional, but the three-course lunch menu is also a great choice. Try the cold cucumber soup or the spring pea soup for starters, then let your taste buds dictate the rest. You can't go wrong in this simply decorated, yet artistically designed restaurant. The food and service are terrific, and the owner takes a personal interest in her guests.

TREATS

To curb a sweet tooth or for an afternoon snack, stop in the **Raleigh Tavern Bakery** (Duke of Gloucester Street, behind the Raleigh Tavern, under $10). They offer a selection of fresh cookies, muffins, rolls, sandwiches, drinks, and other treats. Try the sweet potato muffins and the gingerbread cookies, which are done to perfection and much better than the peanut butter and chocolate chip cookies. Casual seating is available in the courtyard outside. Alcohol must be consumed in the courtyard and cannot be taken out on Duke of Gloucester Street. Recipes are for sale in their cookbook, and this writer knows firsthand that almost nothing has changed in this historical little bakery in the past 30 years, but then again, that's the idea here.

The **Jamestown Pie Company** (1804 Jamestown Rd., 757/229-7775, www.buyapie.com, Sun.-Thurs. 10am-7pm, Fri.-Sat. 10am-8pm, $5-23) sells everything round including pizza, potpie, and dessert pie. They also offer a small selection of sandwiches. Pies are also available to go.

COLONIAL TAVERNS

There are four taverns in the historic area of Williamsburg, and dining in one is a great way to get into the spirit of the town. Costumed

servers bring authentic dishes from two centuries ago to wooden tables in flickering candlelight. Don't be hesitant to try some 18th-century staples such as spoon bread and peanut soup. There are a few featured items available in all four taverns, but aside from that, each specializes in its own dishes. Make reservations when you book your hotel. The same phone number (757/229-2141) can be used for all four taverns. These restaurants are very popular. **Christiana Campbell's Tavern** (101 S. Waller St., Tues.-Sat. at 5pm, $24-35) is noted as George Washington's favorite tavern. It specializes in seafood dishes. The tavern was recreated from artifacts excavated on-site and from a sketch of the building found on an original insurance policy. George and other famous colonial figureheads often met here for business and pleasure, and private rooms could be reserved alongside public chambers where travelers sometimes shared beds with complete strangers when the tavern was full. The crab cakes are a signature dish at the tavern.
Chowning's Tavern (109 E. Duke of Gloucester St., lunch daily 11:30am-3pm, dinner daily 5pm-9pm, lunch $7-13, dinner $24-33) is a casual 18th-century alehouse where lively singing and other character reenactments are common. Light fare is served at Chowning's for lunch, including soups and sandwiches, and more substantial entrées are available for dinner (such as pork and Brunswick stew). Outdoor seating is available behind the tavern in the garden where light meals and pints are served.
The King's Arms Tavern (416 E. Duke of Gloucester St., lunch daily 11:30am-2:30pm, dinner daily from 5pm, $31-37) is a *genteel* tavern serving southern food and decadent desserts. This chop-house-style tavern offers entrées such as chicken, pork chops, venison, and prime rib. The peanut soup is a signature dish.
Shields Tavern (422 E. Duke of Gloucester St., lunch daily 11am-2:30pm, dinner daily 5pm-9pm, $23-29) is the largest of the taverns, and it specializes in comfort food such as bangers and mash and barbecue ribs. Try the

potato leek pie or a sample plate. The ale-potted beef is also a favorite.

Information and Services
The best information on Colonial Williamsburg can be obtained from the **Colonial Williamsburg Foundation** (800/447-8679, www.history.org) and at the **Colonial Williamsburg Regional Visitor Center** (101 Visitor Center Dr., 757/220-7645, daily 8:45am-5pm). For additional information on Williamsburg, contact the **Greater Williamsburg Chamber and Tourism Alliance** (www.williamsburgcc.com) or visit www.visit-williamsburg.com.

Getting There
Most people arrive in Williamsburg by car. The city is off I-64 and approximately 2.5 hours from Washington DC.
The **Newport News/Williamsburg International Airport** (900 Bland Blvd., www.flyphf.com) is off I-64 at exit 255-B. The airport code is PHF. Williamsburg is a 20-minute drive from the airport.
Amtrak (468 N Boundary St., 800/872-7245, www.amtrak.com) offers train service into Williamsburg.

Getting Around
Getting around Colonial Williamsburg requires a lot of walking. The pedestrian area where you'll find many of the attractions is preserved as it was during Revolutionary times when there were no cars. If you are not staying at one of the Colonial Williamsburg hotels, you will want to arrive early during peak season to park outside the pedestrian area. Parking spaces can be difficult to come by, but designated areas are clearly marked. The important thing to remember is not to park in private lots or at the College of William & Mary (even in the summer). Parking restrictions are strictly enforced.
Williamsburg has a reliable bus system called the **Williamsburg Area Transit (WATA)** (www.gowata.org), which offers bus service seven days

a week and services many of the local hotels. An all-day pass is $2.

Shuttle service between the Colonial Williamsburg Regional Visitor Center and select hotels is available for free to those who have a Colonial Williamsburg ticket. Shuttle tickets can also be purchased at the visitor center. From mid-March through October, the **Historic Triangle Shuttle** (www.nps.gov/colo, daily 9am-3:30pm every hour and a half) provides transportation service between the Colonial Williamsburg Regional Visitor Center and Jamestown via the scenic Colonial Parkway. There is no charge if you have purchased a ticket to either historic area. Boarding passes can be obtained from the Colonial Williamsburg Regional Visitor Center.

JAMESTOWN

Jamestown was the first permanent English colony in America, founded in 1607, more than a decade prior to the Pilgrims' arrival at Plymouth. Three small ships carrying 104 men made landfall at Jamestown (which is actually an island) on May 13, 1607. They moored the ships to trees, came ashore the following day, and never left. The newly formed town served as the capital of Virginia during the 17th century.

◖ Jamestown National Historic Site

The original **Jamestown National Historic Site** (1368 Colonial Pkwy., 757/856-1200, www.nps.gov/jame, daily 8:30am-4:30pm, $14) is run by the National Park Service and APVA Preservation Virginia. Purchase your admission ticket at the visitor center (your ticket also grants access to the Yorktown National Battlefield), which shows an informative 18-minute video that is a good start to orienting yourself with the site. From there, continue to "Old Towne," the original settlement site and explore it on foot. Highlights include the original Memorial Church tower (the oldest structure still standing in the park, dating back to 1639), a burial ground (many of the first colonists died here), a reconstructed sample of a "mud-and-stud" cottage, and the foundations of several buildings. Another "don't miss" is the APVA Jamestown Rediscovery excavation, where remains of the original James Fort built in 1607 are being uncovered at an archaeological dig site open to visitors. History programs and children's events are held in the summer months.

Continue on to "New Towne," where you can explore the part of Jamestown that was developed after 1620. The foundations of many homes were excavated in the 1930s and 1950s and replicas can be seen throughout the site. Next, take a drive along the "Loop Drive," a five-mile wilderness road. Be sure to stop to read the interpretive signs and paintings along the route to learn how inhabitants used the island's natural resources, or visit the **Glasshouse** to see artisans creating glass products as glassblowers did back in the early 1600s.

Jamestown Settlement

The **Jamestown Settlement** (2110 Jamestown Rd., 757/253-4838, www.historyisfun.org, daily 9am-5pm, $16) is one of the most popular museums in Coastal Virginia. It is a living museum that recreates and honors the first permanent English-speaking settlement in the country and takes visitors back to the 1600s. Costumed guides share wonderful facts about a Powhatan Village, and replicas of the three ships that sailed from England under the command of Captain Christopher Newport and eventually landed at Jamestown. The ships are a highlight of the museum, and the costumed crew does an excellent job of answering questions and showing off every nook and cranny of the ships. The **James Fort** is another main attraction at the museum. There, visitors can see authentic meals being prepared, witness arms demonstrations, and even try on armor. Ninety-minute tours of the outdoor interpretive areas are available daily at 11am, 1pm, and 3pm. Thanksgiving is a great time to visit as special events are held in the museum. Combined entry tickets to Colonial Williamsburg and the Yorktown Victory Center can be purchased,

A Fair Wind, designed by David Turner, depicts three ship masts and sails at the entrance to the Jamestown Settlement.

© MICHAELA RIVA GAASERUD

and bus service between the sites is offered during the summer season.

Getting There

Jamestown is nine miles southwest of Colonial Williamsburg along the Colonial Parkway.

From mid-March through October, the **Historic Triangle Shuttle** (www.nps.gov/colo, daily 9am-3:30pm every hour and a half) provides transportation service between the Colonial Williamsburg Regional Visitor Center and Jamestown via the Colonial Parkway. There is no charge if you have purchased a ticket to either historic area. Boarding passes can be obtained from the **Colonial Williamsburg Regional Visitor Center** (101 Visitor Center Dr., Williamsburg, 757/220-7645, daily 8:45am-5pm).

YORKTOWN

The quaint waterfront village of Yorktown was established in 1691 and is most famous as the site of the historic victory in the American Revolutionary War. It was also an important tobacco port on the York River where crops were exported from local plantations. During its peak in the mid-1700s, it had nearly 2,000 residents and several hundred buildings. It was a thriving city of primarily merchants, planters, shopkeepers, and indentured servants.

There are many earthworks surrounding Yorktown. These were first built by British troops in 1781, when nearly 80 percent of the town was damaged or destroyed during what is known as the 1781 siege. These earthworks were built over with new fortifications by Confederate troops during the Civil War. During the **Siege of 1862,** the Union army was held back by the Confederates for more than a month in this area. After the Confederates left town, Union troops settled in for the rest of the war.

In addition to learning about history, visitors can enjoy art, shopping, special events, and water sports.

Sights
YORKTOWN NATIONAL BATTLEFIELD AND VISITOR CENTER

The **Yorktown National Battlefield** (757/898-2410, www.nps.gov/yonb) is a national park that marks where, on October 19, 1781, the British army, led by General Charles Lord Cornwallis, surrendered to General George Washington, ending the Revolutionary War. Visitors can see the battlefield, Washington's Headquarters and tent, and the actual surrender field.

The **Yorktown National Battlefield Visitor Center** (1000 Colonial Pkwy., 757/898-2410, reservations 757/898-2411, daily 9am-5pm, $7) is a great place to begin your exploration of the battlefield and town. It is a living history museum, where galleries of films and recreations are discussed by historical interpreters in costume. Two self-guided car tours around the battlefield allow visitors to learn about the history of the Siege of Yorktown at a relaxed pace. Guided group tours are available for $30, and reservations should be made two months in advance.

The entrance fee to the battlefield is paid at the Visitor Center where maps are available as well as an informative orientation film that should be your first order of business if you're a first-timer to the site. The admission fee at Yorktown includes entrance into historic houses, entrance to the battlefield, and access to a variety of interpretive programs and is good for seven days. Your pass can be upgraded to visit Historic Jamestown at the Historic Jamestown Visitor Center for an additional $7.

The 84-foot-tall **Yorktown Victory Monument** and the **Moore House,** where the surrender terms were negotiated, are fascinating sites at the battlefield. The Victory Monument was not erected until 100 years after the end of the war. Its purpose was to "keep fresh in memory the all decisive successes that had been achieved." The four-sided base has an inscription on each side, one for victory, one for a succinct narrative of the siege, one for the treaty of alliance with

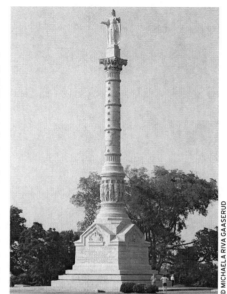

Yorktown Victory Monument

© MICHAELA RIVA GAASERUD

France, and one for the resulting peace treaty with England. The pediments over the inscriptions feature emblems of nationality, war, alliance, and peace. The monument's podium is a "symbol of the birth of freedom." The column (coming out of the podium) symbolizes the greatness and prosperity of the United States after a century. On top of the monument's shaft is a sculpture of Liberty, which attests to the existence of a nation governed by the people for the people.

YORKTOWN VICTORY CENTER

Next to the battlefield is the **Yorktown Victory Center** (Rte. 1020 near Colonial Parkway, 757/253-4838, www.historyisfun.org, daily 9am-5pm with extended summer hours, $9.75), an informative museum dedicated to the American Revolution, which chronicles the entire era beginning with unrest in the colonies and ending with the creation of a new nation. Visitors can view 1,300 artifacts, enjoy artillery demonstrations, explore a re-created Continental army encampment featuring

Yorktown Beach, along the York River

live historical interpreters, and join seasonal celebrations such as the Yorktown Victory Celebration in October honoring the anniversary of the end of the Revolutionary War.

Summer is the best time to visit since there are outdoor living historical exhibits (you might even be asked to help load a cannon). Indoor exhibits are also offered year-round. A free shuttle runs between the Victory Center and historic Yorktown as well as other Williamsburg area attractions. A combination admission ticket for the Yorktown Victory Center and the Jamestown Settlement can be purchased for $20.50.

If you're lucky enough to be here on the Fourth of July, you can experience the **Liberty Celebration** firsthand. What better location to celebrate American's independence than where it all began? The celebration includes a plethora of reenactments, military drills, and food demonstrations. This event complements the **Yorktown Fourth of July Celebration** that takes place in the evening on July 4.

HISTORIC YORKTOWN

Yorktown still has a sparse population of full-time residents. Its streets are lined with historic homes, some more than two centuries old. There's Yorktown Beach, a pleasant sandy beach along the York River, and overall, Yorktown offers a relaxing place to explore history, shop, and dine.

Riverwalk Landing (425 Water St., 757/890-3370, www.riverwalklanding.com) is a pedestrian walkway along the York River. This quaint area includes retail shops and dining. Take a stroll on the mile-long River View that runs along the York River from the Yorktown Battlefield to the Yorktown Victory Center. Riverwalk Landing is a great place to take a walk, go shopping, or grab an ice-cream cone on a hot day.

The **Watermen's Museum** (309 Water St., 757/887-2641, www.watermens.org, Apr.-Thanksgiving Tues.-Sat. 10am-4pm, Sun. 1pm-4pm, Thanksgiving-Mar. Sat. 10am-4pm, Sun. 1pm-4pm, $5) is dedicated to sharing the role that watermen on the Chesapeake

Bay's rivers and tributaries had in the formation of our country. This is done through displays illustrating the methods of their trade and craft. Visitors learn what it means to earn a living harvesting seafood from the Chesapeake Bay's rivers and tributaries. The museum offers educational programs and a waterfront facility that can be rented for events.

The **Nelson House** (Main Street, 757/898-2410, www.nps.gov/york, open as staffing permits, $10) is a prominent 18th-century structure on Main Street. It was built in the Georgian Manor style by the grandfather of Thomas Nelson Jr., one of Yorktown's most famous residents. He was the governor of Virginia in 1781 and the commander of the Virginia militia during the siege in 1781. He was also a signer of the Declaration of Independence. Damage from attacks during the siege is still evident at the Nelson House. Informal tours of the house are available throughout the year. Please call for hours since the house is not open continuously.

Entertainment and Events

The **Lighted Boat Parade** (Yorktown Beach) kicks off the holiday season in early December with a festive boat parade featuring power and sail boats adorned with holiday lights. Musical performances and caroling are held on the beach by the light of a bonfire, and hot cider is served. The event is free to the public.

The **Yorktown Wine Festival** (425 Water St. at Riverwalk Landing) is a free festival featuring wine from throughout Virginia in early October. Art and food vendors also share their wares at the festival.

Shopping

Yorktown's Main Street in the Historic Village is lined with unique shops and galleries. There are antique stores, galleries, and jewelry and glass shops to name a few. Down by the water at the Riverwalk Landing are additional shops featuring colonial architecture and offering art, home items, jewelry, quilts, and clothing.

Sports and Recreation

Yorktown is a waterfront town and outdoor recreation haven. The mile-long **Riverwalk** is a great place for a power walk or to stretch your legs after travel. The two-acre beach near the Riverwalk offers a great location for launching a kayak, swimming, and beachcombing.

There are also kayak and canoe launches at nearby **Wormley Creek Landing** (1110 Old Wormley Creek Rd.) with access to Wormley Creek and the York River, **Rodgers A. Smith Landing** (707 Tide Mill Rd., Tabb) with access to the Poquoson River and the lower Chesapeake Bay, and **New Quarter Park** (1000 Lakeshead Dr., Williamsburg, 757/890-5840, www.yorkcounty.gov) with access to Queens Creek and the York River.

The **Riverwalk Landing Pier** is a pleasant place to enjoy a day of fishing, and visitors can dock their boats there.

For bicycle rentals ($7.50 per hour or $25 for four hours) or guided Segway tours ($39 for one hour or $65 for two hours), contact **Patriot Tours & Provisions** (757/969-5400, www.patriottoursva.com).

If sailing on a romantic schooner sounds appealing, **Yorktown Sailing Charter** (800/979-3370, www.sailyorktown.com, $35 for two hours) docks its beautiful sailing vessel, the schooner *Alliance,* at the pier at Riverwalk Landing April-October. They offer daily sailing trips during the day and at sunset. Daytime trips leave at either 11am or 2pm. Sunset cruise times vary by month. Its sister schooner, *Serenity,* offers pirate cruises (Sun., Mon., Wed., Fri., and Sat. 11:30am-1pm, $35), educational trips, and charters for those looking for a bit of adventure.

Accommodations

The **Duke of York Hotel** (508 Water St., 757/898-3232, www.dukeofyorkmotel.com, $79-190) is an older hotel with a great location right on the water. This family-run establishment has all river-view rooms (some have balconies and some open to landscaped grounds), an outdoor pool, and a café and restaurant

© MICHAELA RIVA GAASERUD

Hornsby House Inn in Yorktown

on-site. The Yorktown Trolley stops in front of the hotel.

The **York River Inn Bed & Breakfast** (209 Ambler St., 757/887-8800, www.yorkriverinn. com, $125-155) sits on a bluff overlooking the York River and offers two rooms, a suite with private bathrooms, and all the hospitality you can imagine from its friendly owner (who is also a knockout breakfast chef). This is a wonderful colonial-style inn with elegant rooms.

The **(** **Hornsby House Inn** (702 Main St., 757/369-0200, www.hornsbyhouseinn.com, $149-189) offers five guest rooms with modern bathrooms in an exquisite historic colonial home. The inn is in the heart of Yorktown and offers a great view of the York River. It is also just a short walk from the Yorktown Battlefield. The inn is run by two warm and friendly brothers who grew up in the house and provide exemplary service and a delicious, fresh breakfast each morning. The house is beautifully appointed and truly a home away from home.

The **Marl Inn Bed & Breakfast** (220 Church St., 757/898-3859, www.marlinnbandb.com,

$109-169) is two blocks from the Riverwalk. This colonial-style home is a private residence and inn offering four guest rooms and continental and full breakfast options. The owner is a great grandson of Thomas Nelson Jr., one of Yorktown's most famous residents.

Food

The **(** **Carrot Tree** (411 Main St., 757/988-1999, www.carrottreekitchens.com, daily lunch, dinner Thurs.-Sat., $9-20) is a delightful historic district restaurant set in Yorktown's oldest home—the Cole Digges House built around 1720. The Carrot Tree offers delicious lunches and equally wonderful dinners with American fare and comfort food. High tea is served on Wednesday. The crab cakes are delicious, but save room for the carrot cake—it's their signature dessert.

The **Riverwalk Restaurant** (323 Water St., 757/875-1522, www.riverwalkrestaurant.net, lunch 11:30am-2:30pm, dinner 5pm-9pm, $13-26) provides diners with a scenic view of the York River through large glass windows and a cozy fireplace for cool evenings. The fare is primarily seafood, but they offer selections from the land as well. This is a great place to relax after at day of sightseeing.

If fresh seafood and cold beer right on the beach sound like a good ending to a day of exploration in Yorktown, stop in at the **Yorktown Pub** (112 Water St., 757/886-9964, www.yorktownpub.com, Mon.-Thurs. 11am-midnight, Fri.-Sun. 11am-1:30am, $7-22). The atmosphere is very casual, but the food and service are good. The pub burger, local oysters, and hush puppies are among the best choices. The place is crowded on the weekends, so plan ahead.

For a quick sandwich, pizza, or burger, stop in the **Beach Delly** (524 Water St., 757/886-5890, Fri.-Mon. 11am-9pm, Tues.-Thurs. 11am-4pm, $8-15). This little restaurant is across from the beach and offers good food and friendly service.

Information and Services
For additional information on Yorktown, visit www.visityorktown.org and www.yorkcounty.gov.

Getting There and Around
Yorktown is 13 miles southeast of Williamsburg along the Colonial Parkway. The **Yorktown Trolley** (www.yorkcounty.gov, daily Mar. 23-May 24 11am-5pm, May 25-Sept. 2

10am-5:30pm, Sept. 3-Nov. 3, 11am-5pm) is a free trolley service with stops in nine locations around Yorktown. It runs every 20-25 minutes from the end of March until November.

JAMES RIVER PLANTATIONS
Between Richmond and Williamsburg (in Charles City County) along Route 5 are four stunning plantations that survived the Revolutionary War, War of 1812, and Civil War. These treasures, which span three centuries, are all privately owned National Register properties that are open to the public. For additional information on all four plantations, visit www.jamesriverplantations.org.

Sherwood Forest
Sherwood Forest (State Route 5, 14501 John Tyler Hwy., Charles City, 804/829-5377, www.sherwoodforest.org, grounds open daily 9am-5pm) sounds like a place out of a fairy tale, and it kind of is. This beautiful plantation was the home of President John Tyler for 20 years. The home has been the residence of the Tyler family continuously since he purchased it in 1842.

At more than 300 feet in length—longer than a football field—Sherwood Forest is the longest frame house in the country. The home evolved from a modest 17th-century English-style home (circa 1660) into a substantial 19th-century "Big House" that features a ballroom

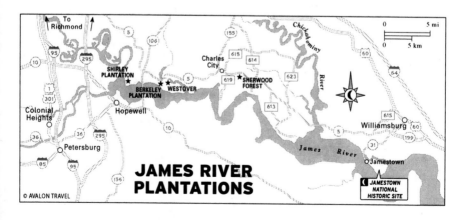

designed specifically for dancers to engage in the Virginia Reel. There is also a resident ghost.

Self-guided walking tours of the grounds are available for $10 per person. The tour features 21 numbered stations on 25 acres with information on the 19th-century plantation. The grounds include terraced gardens, quiet woodlands, and lush lawn. A printed guide is available at a kiosk at the main entrance and features descriptions and history information for each station. House tours are only available by appointment and cost $35.

Westover

Speaking of fairy tales, **Westover** (off Route 5, 804/829-2882, www.jamesriverplantations.org, grounds open daily 9am-6pm, $2) could have come straight off the pages of one. William Byrd II, who founded the city of Richmond, built the home in 1730. Westover is known for its architectural details, but kids of all ages will love it for its secret passages and enchanting gardens. The mansion is widely considered to be one of the top examples of Georgian architecture in the country. The house itself is not open to the public, but there are still many interesting things to see on the grounds, which offer wide views of the James River. The icehouse and another small structure to the east of the mansion contain a dry well and passageways leading under the house and down to the river. These were created as an escape route from the house during attacks. There is a light switch inside the door of each building.

Shirley Plantation

Shirley Plantation (501 Shirley Plantation Rd., 804/829-5121, www.shirleyplantation. com, Mar.-Nov. Mon.-Sat. 9:30am-4:30pm, Sun. 12:30pm-4:30pm, Dec.-Feb. Mon.-Sat. 10am-4pm, Sun. 12:30pm-4pm, $11) was the first plantation built in Virginia. It was founded in 1613, just six years after Jamestown, and

completed in 1738. This property has a legacy of 11 generations of one family (descendants of Edward Hill I) who still own and operate the colonial estate. It has survived attacks, war, and even the Great Depression and remains the oldest family-owned business in the United States.

Admission includes a guided house tour with highlights of original furnishings, artwork, silver, and hand-carved woodwork. Special architectural features include a "flying staircase" and a Queen Anne Forecourt (both are the only examples still in existence in North America). A self-guided grounds tour features gardens and original outbuildings. Allow at least one hour for your visit.

Berkeley Plantation

Berkeley Plantation (12602 Harrison Landing Rd., 804/829-6018, www.berkeleyplantation. com, daily Jan.-mid-Mar. 10:30am-3:30pm, mid-Mar.-Dec. 9:30am-4:30pm, $11) is famous for being the site of the first official Thanksgiving in 1619, although substantiated claims for the first Thanksgiving also belong to locations in Florida, Texas, Maine, and Massachusetts. It is also the birthplace and home of Declaration of Independence signer Benjamin Harrison and President William Henry Harrison. The beautiful Georgian mansion, which was erected in 1726, sits on a hilltop overlooking the James River. The brick used to build the home was fired on the plantation.

Guided tours are conducted in the mansion and feature a nice collection of 18th-century antiques. An audiovisual presentation is included in the tour as is access to a museum collection of Civil War artifacts and unique paintings by artist Sydney King. Visitors can then tour the grounds on their own and explore five terraces of boxwood and flower gardens. Allow approximately 1.5 hours for the house tour and to roam the gardens.

Hampton Roads

The Hampton Roads region is all about water. In sailors' terms, "Roadstead" means a safe anchorage or sheltered harbor. The word "Hampton" came from an English aristocrat, Henry Wriothesley, who was the third earl of Southampton. Hence, Hampton Roads.

Hampton Roads, which used to be known as Tidewater Virginia, contains one of the largest natural deepwater harbors in the world. The harbor is the meeting point of the James, Elizabeth, and Nansemond Rivers with the Chesapeake Bay. Pioneers first settled the area in 1610, after disease struck nearby Jamestown. The area was a throughway for goods from both the colonies and England and, as such, drew merchants and pirates. One of the most famous pirates, Blackbeard (Edward Teach), plundered the port and waters of Hampton Roads, which was just a short distance from his frequented location in North Carolina.

The port in Hampton Roads is the second in size to the country's largest port in New York City and is notable for remaining ice-free year-round. It is also the birthplace of the modern navy.

Defining the Hampton Roads area can be a bit confusing. Technically, the Historic Triangle is considered part of Hampton Roads, but the coastal cities from Newport News to Virginia Beach are more commonly thought of as the Hampton Roads area.

NEWPORT NEWS

Newport News is a short drive from Williamsburg, Virginia Beach, and the Atlantic Ocean. There are several versions of whom Newport News was named for, but the most widely accepted is that it was named for Captain Christopher Newport, who was in charge of the three ships that landed in Jamestown in 1607. The "news" part of the name came from the news that was sent back to England on the ships' safe arrival.

Sights
THE MARINERS' MUSEUM
The Mariners' Museum (100 Museum Dr., 757/596-2222, www.marinersmuseum.org, Mon. and Wed.-Sat. 10am-5pm, Sun. noon-5pm, $12) is one of the largest maritime history museums in the United States. It has more than 60,000 square feet of gallery space showing maritime paintings, artifacts, figureheads, ship models, and small craft from around the world. Exhibits include vessels for warfare, exploration, pleasure, and fishing. A highlight of the museum is the **USS Monitor Center,** where a full-scale replica of the Civil War battleship named the USS *Monitor* is housed. In 1862 the USS *Monitor* battled with the CSS *Virginia* in what went down in history as the first engagement of iron and steam warships (aka The Battle of the Ironclads). Visitors can learn about the historic encounter in the Battle Theater. The center is also home to recovered parts of the original battleship that sank of the coast of Cape Hatteras, North Carolina.

The museum offers countless other collections including the **Crabtree Collection of Miniature Ships.** The museum is very kid-friendly and offers numerous events, lectures, and even a concert series. Check the website for upcoming events.

THE VIRGINIA LIVING MUSEUM
Endangered red wolves, loggerhead turtles, and moon jellyfish are just some of the amazing animals you can get close to at **The Virginia Living Museum** (524 J. Clyde Morris Blvd., 757/595-1900, www.thevlm.org, Mon.-Sun. 9am-5pm, $17). This is a wonderful place to learn about Virginia's natural heritage. Indoor exhibits, outdoor exhibits, four interactive discover centers, and gardens showcase Virginia's geographical regions and the more than 250 species of plants and animals that live there. The 30,000-gallon aquarium containing many sea animals is a focal point for kids of all ages.

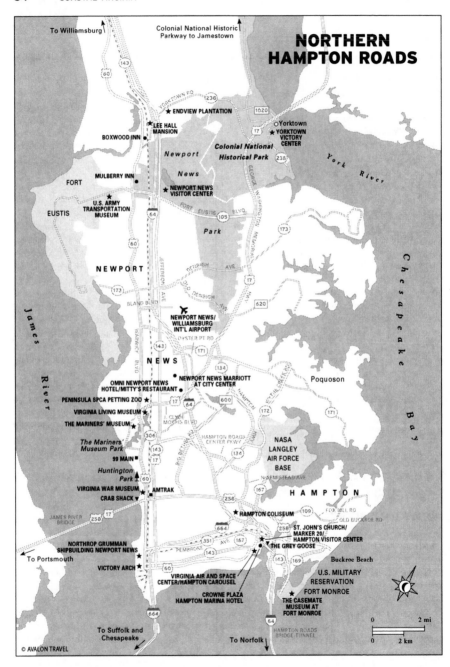

NORTHERN HAMPTON ROADS

To Williamsburg

Colonial National Historic Parkway to Jamestown

★ ENDVIEW PLANTATION

★ LEE HALL MANSION

BOXWOOD INN ●

O Yorktown
★ YORKTOWN VICTORY CENTER

Colonial National Historical Park

Newport

News

York River

MULBERRY INN ●

FORT

★ NEWPORT NEWS VISITOR CENTER

★ U.S. ARMY TRANSPORTATION MUSEUM

EUSTIS

FORT EUSTIS BLVD

Park

NEWPORT

DENBIGH AVE

OLD DENBIGH AVE

BLAND BLVD

✈ NEWPORT NEWS/ WILLIAMSBURG INT'L AIRPORT

OYSTER PT RD

N E W S

Poquoson

OMNI NEWPORT NEWS HOTEL/MITTY'S RESTAURANT ●

★ NEWPORT NEWS MARRIOTT AT CITY CENTER

PENINSULA SPCA PETTING ZOO ★

VIRGINIA LIVING MUSEUM ★

THE MARINERS' MUSEUM ★

J. CLYDE MORRIS BLVD

HAMPTON ROADS CENTER PKWY

NASA LANGLEY AIR FORCE BASE

The Mariners' Museum Park

99 MAIN ■

Huntington Park

N. ARMISTEAD AVE

VIRGINIA WAR MUSEUM ★ ■ AMTRAK

H A M P T O N

CRAB SHACK ▼

FOX HILL RD

OLD BUCKROE RD

JAMES RIVER BRIDGE

★ HAMPTON COLISEUM

NORTHROP GRUMMAN SHIPBUILDING NEWPORT NEWS ★

To Portsmouth

ST. JOHN'S CHURCH/ MARKER 20/ HAMPTON VISITOR CENTER

▼ THE GREY GOOSE

Buckroe Beach

VICTORY ARCH ★

U.S. MILITARY RESERVATION FORT MONROE

VIRGINIA AIR AND SPACE CENTER/HAMPTON CAROUSEL

CROWNE PLAZA HAMPTON MARINA HOTEL

★ THE CASEMATE MUSEUM AT FORT MONROE

To Suffolk and Chesapeake

To Norfolk

HAMPTON ROADS BRIDGE TUNNEL

0   2 mi

0   2 km

James River

Chesapeake Bay

© AVALON TRAVEL

SHIPBUILDING IN NEWPORT NEWS

Newport News is home to the largest privately owned shipyard in the country, **Northrop Grumman Shipbuilding Newport News,** on Washington Avenue along the James River. The facility was originally built in 1886 and was called the Newport News Ship Building and Dry Dock Company. It employed 4,000 people and was poised to repair the many vessels that would use the ever-growing transportation hub in the Hampton Roads area. The shipyard was started with seven million dollars and produced its first tugboat (named Dorothy) in 1891. By 1897, the company had produced three additional tugboats for the U.S. Navy.

With the onset of the Great Naval Race of the early 1900s, business took off. At the start of World War I, the company was in full swing and built six dreadnoughts and 25 destroyers for the U.S. Navy. From that time on, the company has been going full force, even building the first nuclear-powered submarine and the famous passenger ocean liner, the SS *United States*.

Today, the company is the largest private employer in Hampton Roads. The 21,000 employees (of whom many are third and fourth generation shipbuilders) turn raw steel into some of the world's most complex ships. The shipyard is the country's sole designer and builder of nuclear-powered aircraft carriers and also one of only two companies that design and build nuclear submarines.

Many hands-on activities are also offered such as touch tanks and live feedings, and there is even a planetarium.

VIRGINIA WAR MUSEUM

The **Virginia War Museum** (9285 Warwick Blvd., 757/247-8523, www.warmuseum.org, Mon.-Sat. 9am-5pm, Sun. noon-5pm, $6) explains the development of the U.S. military from 1775 to modern times. It offers many exhibits showcasing war efforts throughout our country's history. Weapons, artifacts, and uniforms are displayed from the Revolutionary War through the Vietnam War and exhibits explain the evolution of weaponry, the role of women in the military, contributions made by African Americans to military history, and provide a tribute to prisoners of war.

ENDVIEW PLANTATION

Endview Plantation (362 Yorktown Rd., 757/857-1862, www.endview.org, Apr.-Dec. Mon. and Thurs.-Fri., 10am-4pm, Sat., 10am-5pm, Sun. noon-5pm, Jan.-Mar. Thurs.-Sat. 10am-4pm, Sun. 1pm-5pm, $6) was a privately owned estate that was used briefly as a Confederate hospital during the 1862 Peninsula Campaign. The small, white,

T-frame Georgian-style home was later occupied by federal troops. The house sits on top of a knoll, and a spring flows at the base of the hill. This, coupled with the beautiful rolling farmland that surrounds the place has made it an attractive location for centuries. The city of Newport News purchased the plantation in 1995 and restored it to its original configuration. School programs are held at the plantation, and guided tours of the house and grounds are offered periodically but not on a published schedule.

LEE HALL MANSION

Lee Hall Mansion (163 Yorktown Rd., 757/254-1991, group tours 757/888-3371, www.leehall. org, Mon. and Thurs.-Fri. 10am-4pm, Sat. 10am-5pm, Sun. noon-5pm, $6) is the only remaining large antebellum plantation on the lower Virginia Peninsula. The 6,600-square-foot structure is a blend of several architectural styles, including Italianate, Georgian, and Greek Revival. The primary style, however, is Italianate. The redbrick home was built on a rise in the 1850s and was home to wealthy planter Richard Decatur Lee. Due to the mansion's commanding view, the home served as headquarters for Confederate generals John

Magruder and Joseph E. Johnston during the 1862 Peninsula Campaign. Visitors can take a step back in time to the mid-Victorian period and view hundreds of artifacts in the mansion's authentically furnished rooms. Combination admission tickets for Lee Hall Mansion, Endview Plantation, and the Virginia War Museum can be purchased for $15.

PENINSULA SPCA PETTING ZOO
The **Peninsula SPCA Petting Zoo** (523 J. Clyde Morris Blvd., 757/595-1399, www. peninsulaspca.com, Mon.-Fri. 11am-5:30pm, Sat. 10am-4.30am, $2) is a fun place to bring the kids for a hands-on experience with barnyard animals. The zoo is run by the nonprofit Peninsula Society for the Prevention of Cruelty to Animals (SPCA). Visitors can enjoy the company of sheep, goats, chickens, ducks, and other friendly animals.

VICTORY ARCH
The **Victory Arch** (25th Street and West Avenue, 757/247-8523, www.newport-news. org) was built in 1919. Troops returning from World War I marched through the arch in victory parades after disembarking from their ships. The arch was reconstructed in 1962, and an eternal flame was added to it on Memorial Day in 1969. Today the arch stands as a memorial for all men and women of the armed forces.

Entertainment and Events
FERGUSON CENTER FOR THE ARTS
The **Ferguson Center for the Arts** (1 University Place, 757/594-8752, http://fergusoncenter.cnu.edu) at Christopher Newport University is a performance hall that also houses the university's theater, arts, and music departments. The center opened in 2005 and contains a 1,725-seat concert hall and a 200-seat studio theater. It offers a wide range of performances. Check the website for upcoming events.

PENINSULA FINE ARTS CENTER
The **Peninsula Fine Arts Center** (101 Museum Dr., 757/596-8175, www.pfac-va.

Victory Arch in Newport News

© MICHAELA RIVA GAASERUD

THE PENINSULA CAMPAIGN OF 1862

The Peninsula Campaign of 1862 was an aggressive plan designed by Union forces during the Civil War to outsmart Confederate defenses in Northern Virginia by moving 121,000 troops by sea to the Virginia Peninsula between the York and James Rivers. This would place them to the east of Richmond, the Confederate capital. Having bypassed the Northern Virginia forces, the army, led by General George B. McClellan, would be able to advance to Richmond without meeting entrenched opposition.

The failure of this plan remains a highly debated episode in the war. Union troops moved slowly and never made a serious attack on Richmond, despite their strategic placement. Although they were met by small Confederate forces, McClellan blamed the failure on Washington for not providing men and support for the effort, even though his troops outnumbered the Confederates throughout the campaign.

From the Confederate standpoint, the Peninsula Campaign of 1862 resulted in the emergence of two great commanders, Stonewall Jackson and Robert E. Lee, who jointly kept the Union forces out of Richmond.

org, Tues.-Sat. 10am-5pm, Sun. 1pm-5pm) is a dedicated center for the promotion of the fine arts. It offers exhibits, a studio art school, an interactive gallery, educational programs, and hands-on activities for children.

EVENTS

The **Newport News Fall Festival of Folklife** (www.nngov.com) is held on the first weekend in October and has been going on for approximately four decades. The festival draws 70,000 visitors annually and has more than 230 exhibitors featuring trade demonstrations, crafts, and food.

The **Newport News Children's Festival of Friends** (www.nngov.com) is held at the beginning of May and offers a variety of themed areas for children. Activities, rides, entertainment, and food are all part of the fun of this popular festival that's been going on for more than a quarter century.

Shopping

The **City Center at Oyster Point** (701 Town Center Dr., 757/873-2020, www.citycenteratoysterpoint.com, Mon.-Sat. 10am-9pm, Sun. noon-6pm) is an outdoor town center with retail stores, gourmet eateries, spas, and salons. The **Patrick Henry Mall** (12300 Jefferson Ave., 757/249-4305, www.shoppatrickhenrymall.

com, Mon.-Sat. 10am-9am, Sun. noon-6pm) is the largest mall on the peninsula with more than 120 stores in a single-level, indoor configuration.

Sports and Recreation
PARKS

The **Newport News Park** (13560 Jefferson Ave., 757/886-7912, www.nnparks.com) is one of the largest municipal parks in the country, encompassing 8,000 acres. Boat and bike rentals are available in the park as hiking, biking trails, picnicking, canoeing, archery, disc golf, and fishing. There's a Discovery Center in the park with many hands-on activities and historical artifacts.

Huntington Park-Beach, Rose Garden & Tennis Center (361 Hornet Cir., 757/886-7912) offers a public beach with lifeguards, a playground, baseball, boating, swimming, and tennis. **King-Lincoln Park** (600 Jefferson Ave., 757/886-7912) overlooks the Hampton Harbor and provides fishing, tennis, picnicking, playgrounds, and basketball.

Riverview Farm Park (105 City Farm Rd., 757/886-7912) has two miles of multiuse paved trails, a 30,000-square-foot community playground, biking, hiking, and soccer fields. **The Mariners' Museum Park** (100 Museum Dr., 757/596-2222, www.marinersmuseum.org) offers a five-mile trail along Lake Maury. There is also boating and hiking.

GOLF

Golfers can get their fix at two local courses: **Kiln Creek Golf Club and Resort** (1003 Brick Kiln Blvd., 757/874-2600, www.kilncreekgolf.com, $32-42) and **Newport News Golf Club at Deer Run** (901 Clubhouse Way, 757/886-7922, www.nngolfclub.com, $32-36).

FISHING

Fishing enthusiasts will enjoy the **James River Bridge Fishing Pier** (6701 River Rd., 757/274-0364). At 0.6 mile, it is one of the longest fishing piers on the East Coast.

BOATING

Boaters can make the **Leeward Marina** (7499 River Rd., 757/274-2359, www.nngov.com) a base for exploration of the Hampton Roads Harbor and the Chesapeake Bay.

Accommodations
$100-200

The **Newport News Marriott at City Center** (740 Town Center Dr., 757/873-9299, www.marriott.com, $169-209) is a 256-room hotel near shopping and many restaurants. It offers a pool and workout facility.

The **Comfort Suites Airport** (12570 Jefferson Ave., 757/947-1333, www.newportnewscs.com, $109-145) is the hotel closest to the Newport News/Williamsburg International Airport. It offers all suite accommodations, a free airport shuttle, an indoor pool, and a spacious workout facility.

The **Hilton Garden Inn Newport News** (180 Regal Way, 757/947-1080, http://hiltongardeninn3.hilton.com, $104-144) offers 122 guest rooms, an indoor heated pool and spa, an airport shuttle, and easy access to the city center and military bases.

The **Mulberry Inn** (16890 Warwick Blvd., 757/887-3000, www.mulberryinnva.com, $99-140) is a 101-room hotel offering standard rooms, efficiencies, and studios that can hold up to four people. They provide solid accommodations close to I-64 with amenities such as an outdoor pool, a fitness center, and a business

center. Complimentary continental breakfast is included.

The **Omni Newport News Hotel** (1000 Omni Blvd., 757/873-6664, www.omnihotels.com, $99-209) is only a few blocks from the city center and has a heated indoor pool, a fitness room, and a piano bar. Mitty's Ristorante on-site serves good American/Italian cuisine.

For those seeking more privacy, **The Boxwood Inn** (10 Elmhurst St., 757/888-8854, www.boxwood-inn.com, $105-145) is a historic bed-and-breakfast built in 1897. It offers two rooms and two suites with genuine southern hospitality. Each room in the gracious white home has a theme: The Traveling Saleman's Room is named for the Jewel Tea and Coffee salesman that used to make regular stops at the home; Miss Nana's Room is named for the former owner of the home; the Politician Suite is named for many political gatherings held at the home; and General Pershing's Suite is named for General Pershing who often stayed in the home while on hunting trips. Friday dinners are available by reservation.

Camping

Year-round camping is available in the **Newport News Park** (13564 Jefferson Ave., 757/888-3333, www.nnparks.com, $28.50-31). The park provides 188 campsites with hot showers and restroom facilities.

Food
AMERICAN

C Circa 1918 (10367 Warwick Blvd., 757/599-1918, www.circa1918.com, Tues.-Thurs. 5pm-10pm, Fri.-Sat. 5pm-11pm, $15-25) offers delicious food, a lovely wine list, friendly, professional service, seasonal selections, and wonderful specials. Sample menu items include duck meat loaf, Prince Edward Island mussels, and grilled lamb burgers. The restaurant is in the two-block-long historic Hilton Village neighborhood. The atmosphere is relaxed and comfortable, and separate groups of patrons actually talk to each other. Don't shy away from interacting—you could get a great tip for what to order. This is a small restaurant with only

© MICHAELA RIVA GAASERUD

Circa 1918 restaurant in Newport News

about a dozen tables, so reservations are highly recommended.

Fin Seafood (3150 William Styron Sq., 757/599-5800, www.finseafood.com, daily 11am-10pm, $25-40) is a great choice for a romantic dinner or a large gathering. It is a local favorite for delicious seafood. They use mostly organic and sustainable produce and proteins, as well as seasonal ingredients.

Brickhouse Tavern (141 Herman Melville Ave., 757/223-9531, daily 11am-2am, $7-10) is a casual restaurant serving a variety of pub food, including burgers and pizza. **Chic N Fish** (954 J Clyde Morris Blvd., 757/223-6517, www.chicnfish.com, Mon.-Sat. 11am-9pm, $5-10) serves up a little bit of everything including burgers, fried chicken, and Korean dishes.

One of the best views in town is from the **Crab Shack** (7601 River Rd., 757/245-2722, www.crabshackonthejames.com, Sun.-Thurs. 11am-11:30pm, Fri.-Sat. 11am-12:30am, $8-21) on the waterfront on the James River. This casual seafood restaurant offers visitors sandwiches and entrées in a window-lined dining

room or on an outdoor deck. **Cheeseburger in Paradise** (12361 Hornsby Ln., 757/296-4940, www.cheeseburgerinparadise.com, Mon.-Wed. 11am-midnight, Thurs.-Sat. 11am-1am, Sun. 11am-11pm, $10-15) is a fun family restaurant serving American food with a Caribbean theme.

FRENCH
99 Main (99 Main St., 757/599-9885, www.99mainrestaurant.com, Tues.-Thurs. 5pm-9:30pm, Fri.-Sat. 5pm-10:30pm, $10-25) is considered one of the best establishments for fine-dining in Hampton Roads. The cuisine is "anchored in French classics and technique" and features menu items such as herb-crusted rack of lamb, beef tenderloin, and roasted duck breast. There is a formal dining room and also a bar area.

ITALIAN
For good mid-priced Italian food, try **Al Fresco** (11710 Jefferson Ave., 757/873-0644, www.alfrescoitalianrestaurant.com, lunch Mon.-Fri. 11am-3am, dinner Mon.-Sat. 5pm-10pm, $10-20).

Information and Services
For additional information on Newport News, visit www.newport-news.org or stop by the **Newport News Visitor Center** (13560 Jefferson Ave., 757/886-7777, daily 9am-5pm), off I-64 at exit 250B.

Getting There and Around
Newport News is located along I-64 and U.S. Route 60.

The **Newport News/Williamsburg International Airport** (900 Bland Blvd., www.flyphf.com) is off I-64 at exit 255-B, airport code PHF. Downtown Newport News is a 15-minute drive from the airport.

Amtrak (9304 Warwick Blvd., 757/245-3589, www.amtrak.com) has a station in Newport News at Huntington Park. Consult the website for schedules and fares.

Newport News, Hampton, Norfolk, and Virginia Beach are connected by **Hampton**

Roads Transit (757/222-6100. www.gohrt.com). Consult the website for schedules and fares.

HAMPTON

Hampton is the oldest continuously inhabited, English-speaking community in the United States with a history dating back to 1607. It is also home to Langley Air Force Base. Hampton was partially destroyed during three major wars, the Revolutionary War, the War of 1812, and the Civil War, but was rebuilt each time and continues to undergo renovations even today. The city now offers an attractive waterfront filled with modern sailing and fishing boats and a variety of attractions for visitors and residents.

Sights

VIRGINIA AIR & SPACE CENTER

The **Virginia Air & Space Center** (600 Settlers Landing Rd., 757/727-0900, www.vasc.org, Sept.-Mar. Tues.-Sat. 10am-5pm, Sun. noon-5pm, extended summer hours, $11.50, extra for IMAX) houses more than 100 interactive exhibits that explain the historic achievements of NASA in detail. Topics include space travel, aircraft development, communications, and a hands-on space gallery. Hampton was the birthplace of the space program in the United States and has played an intricate role in the 100-plus-year history of flight. Displays include more than 30 historic airplanes, the Apollo 12 Command Module, a passenger jet, ancient moon rocks, and many replicas.

THE HAMPTON CAROUSEL

The **Hampton Carousel** (Carousel Park, 757/727-0900, www.vasc.org, $2) was originally built for an amusement park at Buckroe Beach, where it resided between 1921 and 1985. It is now on the waterfront in downtown Hampton, fully restored and protected from the elements. The merry-go-round's 48 horses and chariots were hand-carved out of hardwood, and it is adorned with original paintings and mirrors. It also still plays the original organ music. The carousel is open from the end of

© MICHAELA RIVA GAASERUD

the historic Hampton Carousel

March through early September. Normal hours of operation are daily noon-5pm, but it is best to check their website since they have scheduled closures each month.

THE CASEMATE MUSEUM
AT FORT MONROE

The Casemate Museum (20 Bernard Rd., 757/788-3391, www.tradoc.army.mil, daily 10:30am-4:30pm, free), on Fort Monroe, shares many exhibits about the fort, which was built in 1834 to protect the Chesapeake Bay, James River, and Hampton River. This is the largest stone fort in the country and the only fort that is surrounded by a moat. During the Civil War, Fort Monroe was the Union's southernmost fort. The museum contains the prison cell where the Confederate president Jefferson Davis was held and also the living quarters of Robert E. Lee while he was stationed there from 1831 to 1834. Other displays include military uniforms and supplies. The grounds at Fort Monroe are open year-round for walking and other outdoor activities.

ST. JOHN'S CHURCH

St. John's Church (100 W. Queens Way, 757/722-2567, www.stjohnshampton.org) is the oldest English-speaking parish in the United States. The church was founded in 1610, and the current structure was built in 1728. The church was designed in the shape of a Latin cross and boasts beautiful colonial-style brickwork, two-foot-thick walls, and stained glass windows. The church survived the Revolutionary War, the War of 1812, and the Civil War. The silver used for communion dates back to 1618 and is considered to be the most valuable relic in the American Anglican Church. Services are still held here; consult their website for details.

Entertainment and Events

The **Hampton Coliseum** (1000 Coliseum Dr., 757/838-4203, www.hamptoncoliseum.org) is the premier venue in Hampton for concerts, performances, and sporting events. A list of upcoming events can be found on the website.

The coliseum is convenient to I-64 and offers free parking.

Hampton Bay Days (www.baydays.com) is a one of the largest festivals on the East Coast. More than 200,000 people partake in the three-day downtown Hampton event in early September, enjoying music, more than 75 merchandise vendors, and more than 30 food vendors.

The annual **Hampton Jazz Festival** (www.hamptonjazzfestival.com) has been going on for almost 50 years. It is held for three days at the end of June in the Hampton Coliseum. Information on the lineup and tickets can be found on the website.

The **Hampton Cup Regatta** (www.hamptoncupregatta.com) is billed as the "oldest continually run motorsport event in the world." It is held for three days in mid-August. Another fun water festival is the **Blackbeard Pirate Festival** (www.blackbeardfestival.com) held at the beginning of June each year. The Hampton waterfront is overrun with pirate reenactors as visitors are taken back to the seaport of the 18th century. There is live music, children's activities, vendors, fireworks, and arts and crafts.

Sports and Recreation

Buckroe Beach (100 1st St. South) is a wide, sandy, eight-acre beach on the Chesapeake Bay. There is a playground, picnic shelters, a bike path, and certified lifeguards on duty for safe swimming. Concerts are held in the summer months as well as an outdoor family movie series.

Grandview Nature Preserve (State Park Drive) is a local's secret. This nature preserve and beach at the end of Beach Road in Grandview is great for families and allows dogs in the off-season.

Those traveling by boat can stop at the **Blue Water Yachting Center** (15 Marina Rd., 757/723-6774, www.bluewateryachtsales.com). Hampton is located at the entrance to the Chesapeake Bay and serves as the stopping point for many traveling boats and offers daily dockage.

Blue Water Yachting Center in Hampton

If you don't have a boat and wish to take a relaxing sightseeing cruise, board the double-decker *Miss Hampton II* (757/722-9102, www.misshamptoncruises.com, $21 for 3 hours), a motor cruising vessel that offers cruising in Hampton Harbor and on the Chesapeake Bay.

Golf enthusiasts can play at the **Woodlands Golf Course** (9 Woodlands Rd., 757/727-1195, www.hampton.gov, $13-19) or the **Hamptons Golf Course** (320 Butler Farm Rd., www.hampton.gov, $14-21).

Accommodations
UNDER $100
The **Candlewood Suites Hampton** (401 Butler Farm Rd., 877/859-5095, www.candlewoodsuites.com, $82-93) offers 98 reasonably priced, spacious rooms in a quiet location. The hotel is geared toward extended stay guests and offers per diem rates for members of the armed services. The service is good, and the staff is caring and friendly. The rooms are well-stocked, and the hotel is pet-friendly. There are also free laundry facilities on-site.

$100-200
The **Crowne Plaza Hampton Marina** (700 Settlers Landing, 877/859-5095, www.ichotelsgroup.com, $100-164) is a riverfront hotel in downtown Hampton. It is within walking distance to the Virginia Air & Space Center and a short drive to Langley Air Force Base, Fort Monroe, and Northrop Grumman.

The **Embassy Suites Hampton Roads Hotel, Spa and Convention Center** (1700 Coliseum Dr., 757/827-8200, www.embassysuites3.hilton.com, $149-169) offers 295 suites with kitchenettes. The hotel has a warm decor with an attractive atrium, and the staff provides good, reliable service. There's a restaurant and a nicely appointed fitness center on-site. Spa service is also available.

Food
AMERICAN
Surf Rider Bluewater (1 Marina Rd., 757/723-9366, $10-30) is a family-owned seafood restaurant in the Blue Water Yachting Center off Ivy Home Road. This is a great place for

© MICHAELA RIVA GAASERUD

local seafood as you can tell by the number of local residents eating here. Their crab cakes are famous as are the oysters, tuna, and hush puppies.

Another local favorite is **Marker 20** (21 E. Queens Way, 757/726-9410, www.marker20. com, daily 11am-2am, $6-21). This downtown seafood restaurant has a large covered outdoor deck and inside seating. Enjoy a casual menu of soups, salads, sandwiches, and seafood specials, along with dozens of types of beer.

The cute **Grey Goose** (101 W. Queens Way, 757/723-7978, www.greygooserestaurant.com, lunch Mon.-Sat. 11am-3pm, $6-10) serves homemade soups, salads, sandwiches, and bakery items made from fresh ingredients.

SPANISH
The **Six Little Bar Bistro** (6 E. Mellen St., 757/722-1466, www.littlebarbistro.com, daily 5pm-2am, tapas $6-12) serves up an eclectic assortment of tapas including herbed sausage, seaweed salad, pork, and chipotle crab cakes. There is also a large bar that is notorious for mixing good cocktails. The food is delicious, the atmosphere is fun, but they do not split checks, so be prepared for this if you're with a group.

Information and Services
For additional information on Hampton, visit www.hampton.gov and www.visithampton. com or stop in at the **Hampton Visitor Center** (120 Old Hampton Ln., 757/727-1102, Mon.-Sat. 9am-5pm, Sun. 1pm-5pm).

Getting There and Around
Hampton is approximately 10 miles southeast of Newport News.

The **Newport News/Williamsburg International Airport** (900 Bland Blvd., www. flyphf.com) is off I-64 at exit 255-B, airport code PHF. Hampton is a 20-minute drive from the airport.

Greyhound (2 W Pembroke Ave., 757/722-9861, www.greyhound.com) offers bus service to Hampton.

Hampton Roads Transit (www.gohrt. com) is a public transit service that serves the Hampton Roads area including Hampton. It currently offers transportation by bus, light-rail, ferry, and Handi-ride (a service for people with disabilities).

NORFOLK
Norfolk is the second largest city in Virginia and home to the largest naval base in the world. Norfolk is traditionally a Navy town. It has an appealing downtown area and a nice waterfront. The city has undergone a rebirth in recent history that is most evident in the delightful restaurants and shops in the trendy Ghent village. The city also boasts numerous universities, museums, and a host of other attractions including festivals and shopping.

Sights
CHRYSLER MUSEUM OF ART
The **Chrysler Museum of Art** (245 W. Olney Rd., 757/664-6200, www.chrysler.org, Sun. noon-5pm, Wed. 10am-9pm, Thurs.-Sat. 10am-5pm, free) is one of Virginia's top art museums with 62 galleries and 30,000 pieces of artwork including paintings, textiles, ceramics, and bronzes. The art on display spans thousands of years and comes from around the world. A highlight is the glass museum (a museum within a museum) that is entirely devoted to glass art and features 10,000 glass pieces (spanning 3,000 years) and a glass art studio. Other collections include European painting and sculpture, American painting and sculpture, modern art, a gallery of ancient and non-Western art, contemporary art, photography, and decorative arts.

NORFOLK BOTANICAL GARDEN
Something is always in bloom at the **Norfolk Botanical Garden** (6700 Azalea Garden Rd., 757/441-5830, www.norfolkbotanicalgarden. org, Oct. 16-Mar. daily 9am-5pm, Apr.-Oct. 15 daily 9am-7pm, $11). This 155-acre garden contains more than forty different themed areas and thousands of plants. It is open to visitors year-round. Inside the garden is the three-acre **World of Wonders Children's Garden,** which is

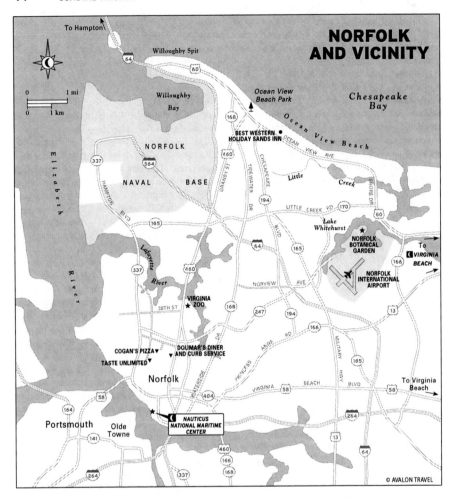

NORFOLK AND VICINITY

To Hampton

Willoughby Spit

Willoughby Bay

Ocean View Beach Park

Chesapeake Bay

BEST WESTERN HOLIDAY SANDS INN

NORFOLK

NAVAL BASE

Ocean View Beach

Little Creek

Lake Whitehurst

NORFOLK BOTANICAL GARDEN

To VIRGINIA BEACH

NORFOLK INTERNATIONAL AIRPORT

VIRGINIA ZOO

COGAN'S PIZZA

DOUMAR'S DINER AND CURB SERVICE

TASTE UNLIMITED

Norfolk

To Virginia Beach

Portsmouth   Olde Towne

NAUTICUS NATIONAL MARITIME CENTER

Elizabeth River

Lafayette River

© AVALON TRAVEL

geared toward children and families and houses several learning areas.

NAUTICUS NATIONAL MARITIME CENTER

The **NAUTICUS National Maritime Center** (1 Waterside Dr., 757/644-1000, www.nauticus. org, daily Memorial Day-Labor Day 10am-5pm, rest of the year Tues.-Sat. 10am-5pm, $13.95) is an incredible interactive science and technology center. They have a great floor plan

with a lot of interesting permanent and rotating exhibits including hands-on activities for children (they will love the Morse code exhibit). Be sure to catch the *Living Sea* movie featured on a large panoramic screen that opens to a view of the water.

The *Battleship Wisconsin* is one of the prime on-site attractions, and the center features many exhibits related to the ship. It is one of the biggest and also one of the last battleships built by the U.S. Navy. The ship served in World

War II, the Korean War, and Operation Desert Storm. Admission to the ship is included with admission to NAUTICUS, and visitors can take a self-guided tour of the deck. For $28.95 (which includes NAUTICUS admission), guided **Battleship Wisconsin Topside Tours** (Tues.-Fri. 11am and 2pm and Sun. 2:30pm) are available. These tours include the administration area, radio room, main deck with enlisted berthing, the captain's cabin and sleeping quarters, the flag bridge, and the combat engagement center. Participants must be at least eight years old and have the ability to climb stairs to four decks and be comfortable in small spaces.

The **Hampton Roads Naval Museum** (free admission) is also located inside the NAUTICUS National Maritime Center on the second floor. The museum is run by the U.S. Navy and features the 237-year history of the Hampton Roads region fleet. Exhibits in the museum include an 18-pounder cannon from 1798, artifacts from the cruiser **CSS Florida** and the sloop-of-war **USS Cumberland**, a World War II Mark 7 undersea mine, and a torpedo warhead from a German submarine.

Allow at least 2-4 hours to explore the center and the ship. There's a casual restaurant on-site serving sandwiches, salads, beverages, and snacks.

NAVAL STATION NORFOLK

Norfolk offers a unique opportunity to tour the largest naval base in the world. The **Naval Station Norfolk** sits on 4,300 acres on Sewells Point and is home to 75 ships and 134 aircraft. The 45-minute bus tour leaves from the **Naval Tour and Information Center** (9079 Hampton Blvd., 757/444-7955, www.norfolkvisitor.com) next to gate 5. The tour rides past destroyers, aircraft carriers, frigates, amphibious assault ships, and the airfield. Tour times change frequently so call for a current schedule.

VIRGINIA ZOO

The **Virginia Zoo** (3500 Granby St., 757/441-2374, www.virginiazoo.org, Mon.-Sun. 10am-5pm, $11) can be found on 53 acres adjacent to Lafayette Park. It opened in 1900 and houses

Virginia Zoo in Norfolk

© MICHAELA RIVA GAASERUD

more than 400 animals including elephants, giraffes, orangutans, otters, and birds. The zoo is operated by the City of Norfolk and the Virginia Zoological Society. It offers many educational and children's programs.

ST. PAUL'S CHURCH

St. Paul's Church (201 St. Paul's Blvd., 757/627-4353, www.saintpaulsnorfolk.com) is the oldest building in Norfolk, dating back to 1739. A cannonball that was fired into the church on the night before the Revolutionary War began is still lodged in its southwestern wall. Tombstones in the church's historic cemetery date back to the 17th and 18th centuries. Episcopalian services are still held at St. Paul's.

Entertainment and Events

Chrysler Hall (215 St. Paul's Blvd., 757/644-6990, www.sevenvenues.com) is the top performing arts venue in the Hampton Roads area. It hosts Broadway shows, concerts, theatrical performances, the **Virginia Symphony** (www.virginiasymphony.org), the **Virginia Arts**

Festival (www.vafest.org), and the **Virginia Ballet.**

The **Virginia Opera** (www.vaopera.org, 866/673-7282) performs in three locations throughout Virginia (Norfolk, Richmond, and Fairfax). The Norfolk venue, the **Harrison Opera House** (160 E. Virginia Beach Blvd.) is a beautifully renovated World War II USO theater, seating just over 1,600 people.

The **Scope Arena** (201 E. Brambleton Ave., 757/644-6990, www.sevenvenues.com) is a 12,000-seat complex that hosts concerts, family shows, and conventions. It is also the home of the **Norfolk Admirals** of the American Hockey League.

Norfolk also has a number of quality small venues featuring good nightlife and entertainment. The **NorVa** (317 Monticello Ave., 757/627-4547, www.thenorva.com), is a 1,500-person concert venue featuring a variety of artists such as Ingrid Michaelson, Citizen Cope, and The Legwarmers. **The Banque** (1849 E. Little Creek Rd., 757/480-3600, www.thebanque.com) is a popular, award-winning country-and-western nightclub and restaurant offering a large dance floor and well-known artists.

Norfolk Festevents (757/441-2345, www.festevernts.org) presents more than 65 days of events including concerts and festivals in **Town Point Park** (on the Elizabeth River in the center of the business district in downtown Norfolk) and **Ocean View Beach Park** (at the end of Granby Street at Ocean View Avenue) February through October. One of the most popular events, the **Norfolk Harborfest** is held annually for four days at the beginning of June and attracts more than 100,000 people. This large festival covers more than three miles on the Norfolk waterfront and offers visitors three sailboat parades, tall ships, the largest fireworks display on the East Coast and seemingly endless entertainment. Another Festevent, the **Norfolk Jazz Festival** is a three-day festival held in mid-July. Tickets range from $38-58 for the weekend. The **Town Point Virginia Wine Festival** is held in Town Point Park for two days in October. More than 200 Virginia wines are featured. Tickets are required.

Shopping

The **Waterside Festival Marketplace** (333 Waterside Dr.) is a bustling shopping area with dozens of stores, restaurants, art exhibits, and live entertainment. The marketplace opened in the early 1980s as part of a revitalization of the area. The **Waterside Marina** is within walking distance and offers boat tours and ferry service.

The **MacArthur Center** (300 Monticello Ave., 757/627-6000, www.shopmacarthur.com, Mon.-Sat. 10am-9pm, Sun. noon-6pm) is a large shopping mall with close to 150 retail stores and restaurants. There is also a movie complex.

A trendy little shopping area worth checking out is **The Palace Station & Shops of Ghent** (Llewellyn Avenue and 21st Street, www.palacestationofghent.com) in the historic Ghent neighborhood. Thirty-five unique shops and restaurants line the retail shopping complex near downtown Norfolk. Boutiques, antiques stores, gift stores, and craft stores are just some of the establishments found in this interesting area.

Sports and Recreation

Harbor Park (www.milb.com), is home to the AAA **Norfolk Tides.** The park is considered to be one of the best minor league baseball facilities in the country with its practical design and terrific view in downtown Norfolk. The park opened in 1993 on the Elizabeth River.

The **Norfolk Admirals** (www.norfolkadmirals.com) take to the ice seasonally at the **Scope Arena** to compete in the American Hockey League. Consult the website for schedules and tickets.

Those looking for a little local adventure can take in a **sand wrestling** (www.sandwrestling.com) competition. Sand wrestling, which is also known as beach wrestling, is an ancient version of the sport of wrestling. Established as an international style of amateur wrestling in 2005, it is quickly gaining popularity and offers competition for males and females of all ages.

Beachgoers can enjoy miles of public beach at **Ocean View Beach Park** (www.norfolk.gov). The park offers a boardwalk, bandstand, beach access ramp for people with disabilities, commercial fishing pier, and open recreation space. There is a bathhouse, and parking is free. Dogs are allowed on leashes in the off-season.

A trip with **American Rover Sailing Cruises** (333 Waterside Dr., 757/627-7245, www.americanrover.com, $18) is a relaxing way to tour the Hampton Roads Harbor and the Elizabeth River. The American Rover's red sails are a distinguishing sight in the Hampton Roads area. From April through October, they offer 1.5- and 2-hour narrated cruises. Guests can help out with sailing the ship or just sit back and relax.

Accommodations
UNDER $100
The **Tazewell Hotel & Suites** (245 Granby St., 757/623-6200, www.thetazewell.com, $94-140) is a reasonably priced historic hotel offering 58 guest rooms and suites. The hotel was built in 1906 and is conveniently located downtown near many sites and businesses.

$100-200
There are many chain hotels in Norfolk. A few stand out for above average accommodations, good service, and proximity to downtown attractions and the airport, such as the **Courtyard Norfolk Downtown** (520 Plume St., 757/963-6000, www.marriott.com, $159-179), the **Holiday Inn Express Hotel & Suites Norfolk International Airport** (1157 N. Military Hwy., 877/859-5095, www.hiexpress.com, $135-175), and the **Residence Inn Norfolk** (227 W. Brambleton Ave., 888/236-2427, www.marriott.com, $169-249).

In addition to the selection of large chain hotels, there are some very nice bed-and-breakfasts and historic hotels in Norfolk. The **Page House Inn** (323 Fairfax Ave., 757/625-5033, www.pagehouseinn.com, $145-230) is a historic bed-and-breakfast (circa 1899) next to the Chrysler Museum of Art in the Ghent Historic District. This stately redbrick mansion has four guest rooms and three guest suites, decorated with 19th-century furniture, antiques, and art. A delicious full breakfast is served each morning, and refreshments are served each afternoon. The innkeepers are warm and welcoming.

The **(Freemason Inn and Breakfast** (411 W. York St., 757/963-7000, www.freemasoninn.com, $155-195) is known for its tasteful interior, spacious rooms, comfortable beds, and incredible food (they serve a three-course breakfast). Four elegant guest rooms and a friendly host make this a top choice in Norfolk. The inn is centrally located near the harbor but in a charming neighborhood.

Food
AMERICAN
(Freemason Abbey Restaurant (209 W. Freemason St., 757/622-3966, www.freemasonabbey.com, Mon.-Thurs. 11am-9:30pm, Fri.-Sat. 11am-10:30pm, Sun. 9:30am-9:30pm, $16-27) is a local favorite in downtown Norfolk for fresh seafood, steak, and pasta. It is housed in a 140-year-old renovated church and has been a restaurant for more than two decades. The atmosphere is friendly, elegant, and casual with a beautiful decor that retains a church-like feel yet has cozy seating. Try the award-winning She Crab Soup. Reservations are highly recommended on the weekends.

Doumar's Diner & Curb Service (1919 Monticello Ave., 757/627-4163, www.doumars.com, Mon.-Thurs. 8am-11pm, Fri.-Sat. 8am-midnight, $2-4) is a legendary diner that was featured on the show *Diners, Drive-Ins and Dives*. Its origin was an ice-cream stand that opened in 1907 in Ocean View Amusement Park. The business moved to its current location in 1934 and is still owned by the same family. Famous for barbecue and ice cream, they still bake their own ice-cream cones in the original cone machine. Take a seat inside the diner, or dine from your car and enjoy their car-hop service. This is a fun, genuine, old-school diner that is inexpensive and has a great history.

Seafood lovers can get their fix at **A. W. Schuck's** (2200 Colonial Ave., 757/664-9117,

© MICHAELA RIVA GAASERUD

Doumar's Diner & Curb Service in Norfolk

daily 11am-1:30am, $8-15). They seem to be firm believers that any meal can include seafood. Try their burger topped with lump crab or a po'boy, both are well seasoned, huge, and delicious. Finding the place can be a bit tricky—look on 22nd Street in the plaza rather than Colonial Avenue. The staff is friendly and attentive, and the atmosphere is social. This is a good choice for reasonably priced, yet tasty food.

ITALIAN
Razzo (3248 E. Ocean View Ave., 757/962-3630, www.razzo-norfolk.com, daily from 5pm, $8-16) is a big hot spot in a small package. This tiny Italian restaurant on Ocean View only has a handful of tables, but waiting for one

is worth your time (and there's a well-stocked bar that can make that wait more enjoyable). The food is outstanding with daily specials and homemade bread. When in doubt, order the chicken marsala.

Information and Services
For additional information on the Norfolk area, visit www.visitnorfolktoday.com.

Getting There and Around
Norfolk is 16 miles south of Hampton.

The **Norfolk International Airport** (www.norfolkairport.com, code ORF) is convenient for those traveling by air to the Norfolk area. It is one mile east of I-64 (exit 279) and just minutes from downtown Norfolk.

The city is serviced by **Amtrak** (130 Park Ave., www.amtrak.com) rail service and by **Greyhound** (701 Monticello Ave., 757/625-7500, www.greyhound.com) bus service.

Norfolk Electric Transit (www.gohrt.com) is part of Hampton Roads Transit and offers free bus service around town and stops at major attractions. It operates weekdays 6am-6:15pm at 15-minute intervals and 6:15pm-11pm at 30-minute intervals. Saturday service is 6am-12:15am at 30-minute intervals, and Sunday service is 7am-11:15pm at 30-minute intervals.

Hampton Roads Transit also offers **Paddlewheel Ferry** (www.gohrt.com, $1.50) service on three passenger paddle-wheel boats. Each boat holds 150 passengers and runs between downtown Norfolk (at the Waterside) and Portsmouth. The ferry operates every half hour Monday-Thursday 7am-9:45pm, Friday 7am-11:45pm, Saturday 10am-11:45pm, and Sunday 10am-9:45pm. Extended service kicks in during peak summer weeks. Passengers are allowed to bring bicycles on board.

Virginia Beach

Virginia Beach is the premier beach destination in the state. It is a thriving town year-round with more than 437,000 full-time residents and an influx of nearly three million visitors annually. Everyone coming to town is greeted by **King Neptune,** a 24-foot-tall statue that stands on the boardwalk. He is a sign that this is not a quiet beach village, but rather a bustling tourist destination with sand, surf, ice cream, cotton candy, and funnel cake. The resort area runs along more than 20 miles of beach, which is maintained and refurbished on a regular basis. The area is booming with commercialism and has more than its share of touristy gift shops and oversize hotels, but also offers a variety of attractions, events, parks, and wildlife refuges. The farther north you travel, the quieter it gets, and the northern reaches are mostly residential.

The three-mile-long boardwalk is the center of activity, and the aquarium, water sports, fishing, and parks keep visitors coming back year after year. Accommodations are plentiful but also book quickly during the peak summer season, especially those right on the beach. The beach is busiest not only in the summer but also during March and April, when thousands of college students arrive for spring break. Keep this in mind when planning your trip since it may be best to avoid these windows unless you are joining in the fun.

Tourism in Virginia Beach began with the opening of the first hotel in 1884. The boardwalk was built just four years later. The strip has been growing ever since, and a few historic landmarks such as the Cavalier Hotel (circa 1927) still stand today.

A population boom in the 1980s resulted in some bad press for the beach area, which experienced some pains from the onslaught of visitors and the hard partying that came with

© MICHAELA RIVA GAASERUD

Virginia Beach's resort area runs along more than 20 miles of beach.

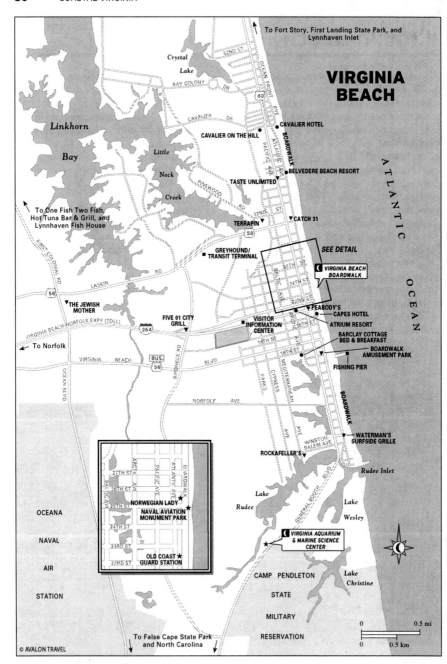

To Fort Story, First Landing State Park, and
Lynnhaven Inlet

Crystal
Lake

**VIRGINIA
BEACH**

Linkhorn

Bay

Little

Neck

Creek

CAVALIER HOTEL
CAVALIER ON THE HILL
BELVEDERE BEACH RESORT
TASTE UNLIMITED

To One Fish Two Fish,
Hot Tuna Bar & Grill, and
Lynnhaven Fish House

TERRAPIN ▼   ▼ CATCH 31

GREYHOUND/
TRANSIT TERMINAL

SEE DETAIL

VIRGINIA BEACH
BOARDWALK

THE JEWISH
MOTHER

FIVE 01 CITY
GRILL

VISITOR
INFORMATION
CENTER

▼ PEABODY'S
CAPES HOTEL
ATRIUM RESORT
BARCLAY COTTAGE
BED & BREAKFAST
BOARDWALK
AMUSEMENT PARK
FISHING PIER

To Norfolk

BOARDWALK

▼ WATERMAN'S
SURFSIDE GRILLE

ROCKAFELLER'S ▼

Rudee Inlet

Lake
Rudee

Lake
Wesley

OCEANA

NAVAL

AIR

STATION

27TH ST
26TH ST
25TH ST
NORWEGIAN LADY ★
NAVAL AVIATION
MONUMENT PARK ★
24TH ST
23RD ST
22ND ST
OLD COAST ★
GUARD STATION

Lake
Christine

VIRGINIA AQUARIUM
& MARINE SCIENCE
CENTER ★

CAMP PENDLETON

STATE

MILITARY

RESERVATION

To False Cape State Park
and North Carolina

ATLANTIC

OCEAN

0   0.5 mi

0   0.5 km

© AVALON TRAVEL

them. Since then, the municipality has made a large effort and spent millions of dollars to revamp the beach's reputation as a family resort. They've succeeded on most levels by encouraging more high-end businesses to come to the beach and by making the main thoroughfares more visually pleasing to visitors with fresh lighting and landscaping. The area is now known for its excellence in environmental health, and as more and more sporting events are booked for the beach, it is becoming a destination for the fitness-minded. In a nutshell, Virginia Beach is a modern and affordable vacation destination that offers a little bit of everything.

SIGHTS

◖ Virginia Beach Boardwalk

No trip to Virginia Beach is complete without a stroll along the 28-foot-wide boardwalk running parallel to the ocean for three miles (between 1st Street and 42nd Street) on one of the longest recreational beach areas in the world. The boardwalk is perfect for getting some exercise with a view. There are lanes for walkers and bicycles, and many running events utilize a portion of the boardwalk on their route, including the **Shamrock Marathon** (www.shamrockmarathon.com) and the **Rock 'n' Roll Marathon Series** (www.runrocknroll.competitor.com). The boardwalk is adorned with benches, grassy areas, play areas, amusement parks, arcades, hotels, restaurants, shops, and other entertainment. There is also a large fishing pier at 15th Street.

Some special features along the boardwalk include the **Naval Aviation Monument,** which stands at 25th Street and pays tribute to the navy, marine corp, and coast guard. Nearby is the **Norwegian Lady** statue that commemorates the lives lost during the shipwreck of a boat from Moss, Norway (a sister statue was erected in Moss). At 13th Street is the **Virginia Legends Walk,** a landscaped walkway that pays tribute to some of Virginia's most famous citizens, including Thomas Jefferson, Robert E. Lee, Captain John Smith, Ella Fitzgerald, and Arthur Ashe.

There are public restrooms at 17th, 24th, and 30th Streets.

◖ Virginia Aquarium & Marine Science Center

The **Virginia Aquarium & Marine Science Center** (717 General Booth Blvd., 757/385-3474, www.virginiaaquarium.com, daily 9am-6pm, $27) is a "don't miss" attraction in Virginia Beach. With its more than 800,000 gallons of aquariums, live animal habitats, hundreds of exhibits, an outdoor aviary, and a 3D IMAX Theater, you could spend several hours or an entire day here and not get bored. Visitors are taken through a "Journey of Water" that introduces them to native plants and animals that live in the Virginia's waterways. There are many hands-on experiences in the center, including a touch pool of friendly stingrays that are eager to be petted by little hands. There's a wonderful nature trail on-site where you can see river otters and ospreys. An expansion exhibit called "Restless Planet" put together in 2009 departs from Virginia's animal kingdom to showcase species from other parts of the world such as Komodo dragons and cobras. This is a wonderful attraction when you need a break from the beach, and kids of all ages find it compelling.

Old Coast Guard Station

The **Old Coast Guard Station** (2401 Atlantic Ave., 757/422-1587, www.oldcoastguardstation.com, Mon.-Sat. 10am-5pm, Sun. noon-5pm, $4) houses more than 1,800 artifacts and 1,000 photographs that honor Virginia's maritime heritage. Two galleries preserve the history of the U.S. Life-Saving and Coast Guard Services, along with shipwrecks off the Virginia coast. The building itself was constructed in 1903 and is the only one of five original life-saving stations built that year along the Virginia coast that remains standing. It now resides on the boardwalk at 24th Street, and a rooftop "Towercam" enables guests to look at ships in the Atlantic.

© MICHAELA RIVA GAASERUD

The Old Cape Henry Lighthouse

The Old Cape Henry Lighthouse

The Old Cape Henry Lighthouse (583 Atlantic Ave., Fort Story, 757/422-9421, www.preservationvirginia.org, Mar. 16-Oct. 31 daily 10am-5pm, Nov. 1-Mar. 15 daily 10am-4pm, $5) is part of the Fort Story Military Base. It once protected the entryway to the Chesapeake Bay at the northern end of Virginia Beach. Construction of the lighthouse was authorized by George Washington as one of the first acts of the newly organized U.S. federal government and the first federal construction project. Alexander Hamilton oversaw its construction. The lighthouse was completed in 1792. This octagonal sandstone edifice remains one of the oldest surviving lighthouses in the country and is a National Historic Landmark. Visitors can climb to the top of the lighthouse and enjoy commanding views of the Chesapeake Bay and the Atlantic Ocean. Guided tours of the grounds are also available, and there's a gift shop on-site. To reach the lighthouse, you must drive through a security gate at Fort Story. Photo identification is required to enter, and car searches are frequently made.

ENTERTAINMENT AND EVENTS

Endless entertainment can be found on the Virginia Beach boardwalk, including concerts, athletic events, and performances.

Nightlife

Virginia Beach doesn't sleep when the sun goes down. In fact, in the summer it doesn't seem to sleep at all. Live music can be found at the **Hot Tuna Bar & Grill** (2817 Shore Dr., 757/481-2888, www.hottunavb.com, daily from 4pm). They offer Top 40 dance music starting at 10pm. Another dance bar is **Peabody's** (209 21st St., 757/422-6212, www.peabodysvirginiabeach.com). They've been around since 1967 and have one of the largest dance floors in the area.

If a game of pool is more your speed, try **Q-Master II Billiards** (5612 Princess Anne Rd., 757/499-8900, www.q-masters.com). They are the premier billiards room in the region and have 72 tables. They also host competitions.

For those wishing to kick back for some live folk, jazz, or blues, stop in **The Jewish Mother** (600 Nevan Rd., 757/428-1515, www.jewishmother.com). They offer live entertainment and a large menu that includes delicious deli sandwiches. If comedy is more up your alley, catch a show at the **Funny Bone Comedy Club & Restaurant** (217 Central Park Ave., 757/213-5555, www.vabeachfunnybone.com). They host well-known comics and offer tables with a full dinner and bar menu during the show. Shows are for ages 21 and older.

Events

Some popular annual events include the **American Music Festival** (5th Street and Atlantic Avenue, www.beachstreetusa.com, $35), the largest outdoor music event held on the East Coast. It runs for three days over Labor Day weekend and features local and national artists. Sounds of rock, jazz, country, blues, and R&B flow out to the oceanfront from a huge stage on the beach at 5th Street and from stages in many parks along the water. Another favorite is the **Boardwalk Art Show and Festival** (http://virginiamoca.org) held annually for four days in mid-June. This event began in 1956 and is one of the oldest and best outdoor art shows on the East Coast. It is held on the boardwalk between 17th Street and 24th Street.

Runners won't want to miss the annual **Shamrock Marathon** (www.shamrockmarathon.com) weekend in mid-March. The Shamrock Marathon has been around since 1973 and is now a premier running event with more than five races over the weekend and 24,000 participants.

SPORTS AND RECREATION
Parks and Wildlife
First Landing State Park (2500 Shore Dr., 757/412-2300, www.first-landing-state-park. org, daily 8am-dusk, $5) is the site where the first permanent English settlers landed in 1607. This 2,888-acre park offers 20 miles of hiking trails, biking, fishing, a boat ramp, and camping.

Mount Trashmore Park (310 Edwin Dr., 757/473-5237, www.vbgov.com, 7:30am-dusk, free) is a famous land-reuse park that was built on an old landfill. The 165-acre park was created by compressing multiple layers of waste and clean soil. The park includes playgrounds, picnic areas, volleyball courts, and a large skating park.

Back Bay National Wildlife Refuge (4005 Sandpiper Rd., 757/301-7329, www.fws.gov/backbay, daily during daylight hours, $5) includes approximately 9,000 acres of beach, marsh, and woods. It is a haven for many migratory birds. There is both fresh and saltwater fishing, a canoe and kayak launch, biking, and hiking. **False Cape State Park** (4001 Sandpiper Rd., 757/426-7128, www.virginiastateparks.gov, 24 hours) is an ocean-to-brackish water area that is only accessible by boat, bike, or on foot. The land trail leading in is five miles long. A tram from the Back Bay National Wildlife Refuge visitor center is also available (call for a schedule). Primitive camping is allowed.

Boat Ramps
The **Owl Creek Boat Ramp** (701 General Booth Blvd.) is a free launch facility next to the Virginia Aquarium & Marine Science Center. Other boat ramps include **First Landing State Park** (2500 Shore Dr., www.virginiastatparks. gov), **Bubba's Marina** (3323 Shore Dr., www. bubbasseafoodrestaurant.com), and **Munden Point Park** (2001 Pefley Ln., www.vbgov. com/parks).

Kayaking and Boat Tours
There are many local outfitters in the Virginia Beach area offering seasonal kayak tours, rentals, and eco-tours. **Chesapean Outdoors** (757/961-0447, www.chesapean.com) provides an exciting guided dolphin kayak tour ($60) where guests can paddle with bottlenose dolphins at the north end of Virginia Beach. They also offer guided sunset paddle tours ($55) and rentals (single kayak, half day $25, full day $40; tandem kayak, half day $35, full day $50). **Kayak Nature Tours** (757/480-1999, www.tidewateradventures. com) also has guided dolphin kayak tours (2.5 hours, $60), flat-water guided trips (2.5 hours, $50), and rentals (single, all day $45; tandem, all day $65).

Explore the creeks near the **Virginia Aquarium & Marine Science Center** (www.virginiaaquarium.com) on a guided pontoon boat or ride along with the aquarium on a 90-minute seasonal dolphin-watching excursion ($21). The aquarium also offers ocean collections boat trips, when a variety of sea creatures are brought on board, and winter wildlife boat trips (75 minutes, $19).

Kayaking tours are available through **Chesapean Outdoors** (757/961-0447, www. chesapean.com, $55), **Back Bay Getaways** (757/721-4484, www.backbaygetaways.com, $35-45), **Kayak Nature Tours, Ltd.** (757/480-1999, www.kayaknaturetours.net, $50-115), and **Ocean Eagle Kayak** (757/589-1766, www. oceaneaglekayak.com, $75).

THE GREAT DISMAL SWAMP

The **Great Dismal Swamp National Wildlife Refuge** (3100 Desert Rd., Suffolk, free) is a 112,000-acre refuge southwest of Virginia Beach. The refuge is primarily forested wetlands and home to numerous birds and animals. It also encompasses 3,100-acre Lake Drummond, which is the largest natural lake in Virginia. One hundred miles of trails are open daily in the refuge for hiking, walking, and biking (sunrise to sunset).

Although humans first occupied the swamp area as much as 13,000 years ago, there was not much interest in the area until Lake Drummond was discovered by William Drummond (a governor of North Carolina) in 1665. The area was later surveyed, and the state line between Virginia and North Carolina was drawn through it in 1728. The name of the land was recorded as the Great Dismal (dismal was a common term at the time for a swamp). Shortly thereafter, George Washington visited the swamp and developed the Dismal Swamp Land Company in an effort to drain and log parts of it. The name "great" was likely added to the swamp's name due to its large size. Logging continued in the swamp until 1976, with all parts of the swamp having been logged one or more times.

The dense forests in the swamp have traditionally been a refuge for animals, but was also used by people for a similar reason. The swamp was at one time a haven for fleeing slaves, and as a result, the swamp was the first National Wildlife Refuge to be recognized officially as part of the Underground Railroad.

Today, more than 200 species of birds live in the refuge either permanently or seasonally. Perhaps an even more impressive fact is that 96 species of butterflies have also been recorded here. More than 47 mammals live in the refuge, including black bears, bobcats, white-tailed deer, river otters, and mink.

For more information, visit www.fws.gov/refuge or contact the park headquarters at 757/986-3705.

Fishing

The Virginia Beach coastline and inshore waterways are thoroughfares for many species of fish including tuna, bluefin, blue marlin, Atlantic mackerel, red drum, and flounder. Private fishing charters are available through a number of companies including **Bubba's Marina and The Shellfish Company** (3323 Shore Dr., 757/481-3513, www.bubbasseafoodrestaurant.com), **Dockside Seafood and Fishing Center** (3311 Shore Dr., 757/481-4545, www.fishingvabeach.com), **Rudee Inlet Charters** (200 Winston Salem Ave., 757/425-3400, www.rudeeinletcharters.com), **Virginia Beach Fishing Center** (200 Winston Salem Ave., 757/491-8000, www.virginiafishing.com), and **Fisherman's Wharf Marina** (524 Winston Salem Ave., 757/428-2111, www.fishermanswharfmarina.com).

There are also several fishing piers that are great for dropping a line such as the **Virginia Beach Fishing Pier** (15th Street), the **Little Island Fishing Pier** (3820 S. Sandpiper Rd., www.sandbridgepier.com), the **Lynnhaven Fishing Pier** (2350 Starfish Rd., www.lynnhavenpier.com), and the **Sea Gull Fishing Pier** at the Chesapeake Bay Bridge-Tunnel (www.cbbt.com).

Amusement Park

The **Boardwalk Amusement Park** (233 15th St., www.virginiabeach.com) has a yesteryear vibe that is nostalgic for parents and pure fun for the kiddies. A Ferris wheel and other stomach-turning rides including its famous Skyscraper, which soars 165 feet in the air at 65 miles per hour, are part of the package. Pricing for the rides varies. Wristbands can be purchased for unlimited rides on one day and are priced according to what time you arrive at the park. The Skyscraper is the only exception, which is always an additional fixed price of $20.

ACCOMMODATIONS

$100-200

The **Belvedere Beach Resort** (3603 Atlantic Ave., 800/425-0612, www.belvederebeachresort.com, $175-200) is a privately owned hotel on the oceanfront on the northern end of Virginia Beach. The light-filled, wood-paneled rooms offer private balconies with views of the beach. The hotel has adult-size bicycles for guest use and direct access to the boardwalk. Rooms are quiet, and the staff is very friendly and helpful. The **Wave Trolley** stops in front of the hotel for easy access to many places on the beachfront. This is not a luxurious resort, but a very pleasant, comfortable choice in a fantastic location. The hotel is open seasonally, normally April through the beginning of October. Minimum stays may be required. Coffeepots are available upon request.

$200-300

The **Capes Hotel** (2001 Atlantic Ave., 757/428-5421, www.capeshotel.com, $192-277) is a pleasant oceanfront hotel on the boardwalk. It has an indoor pool with a view of the ocean and nicely kept grounds. The hotel is convenient to all the beach attractions. The 59-oceanfront rooms are cozy rather than large, but all are comfortable with an airy feel and good views. The service is also very dependable. There is a small café on-site with an oceanfront patio. This is not a luxurious resort, but it doesn't attempt to be; it's a good value in a great location, with a friendly staff.

The **Cavalier Hotel** (4201 Atlantic Ave., 757/425-8555, www.cavalierhotel.com, $159-249) is a historic hotel that first opened in 1927. The original hotel was built up on a hill overlooking the ocean and still welcomes guests during the peak summer season (June 15-Labor Day) as the Cavalier on the Hill. This stately brick landmark portrays the bygone age of grand hotels and sits majestically above the hubbub of activity on the oceanfront. The rooms are traditionally decorated with wood furnishings and lavish window treatments to reflect the era of the hotel's heyday. The 18-acre property also contains the contemporary Cavalier Oceanfront. The oceanfront accommodations are modern and luxurious and provide ocean-view and oceanfront guest rooms. There are around 300 rooms between the two buildings. Guests of both hotels have access to modern amenities such as pools and a large fitness room.

The **Atrium Resort** (315 21st St., 800/955-9700, www.vsaresorts.com, $250-330) is a comfortable hotel a few blocks from the boardwalk. They offer 90 suites with well-appointed kitchenettes, an open-air lobby, and a small indoor pool. The rooms are well-kept, with updated televisions and comfortable beds. The hotel is owned by VSA Resorts, along with two others in Virginia Beach (Ocean Sands Resort and the Ocean Key Resort). They offer room rentals and vacation ownership (similar to a timeshare). Grocery deliver is available upon request. Orders can be placed online and delivered to your room upon arrival.

Over $300

The imposing 21-story **Hilton Virginia Beach Oceanfront** (3001 Atlantic Ave., 757/213-3000, www3.hilton.com, $349-585) offers oceanfront luxury with amenities such as a rooftop infinity pool, a heated indoor lap pool, a Sky Bar, fully equipped fitness center, and spa. There are 289 modern rooms and suites, decorated with a blue and green beach decor and 37-inch televisions. There are several restaurants on-site and convenient parking ($8 for self-park and $16 for valet per day).

Bed-and-Breakfasts and Inns

The **Barclay Cottage Bed and Breakfast** (400 16th St., 757/422-1956, www.barclaycottage.com, $170-250) is a beautiful B&B offering five comfortable guest rooms. Three rooms have private bathrooms, and two offer shared bath facilities. Each room is individually decorated with its own colors and theme (such as nautical or floral). The white, two-story, porch-wrapped cottage (complete with rocking chairs) is within walking distance of many attractions and a few blocks from the beach.

The **Country Villa Bed and Breakfast**

(2252 Indian River Rd., 757/721-3844, www.countryvillainn.com, $169-389) is a charming B&B on four acres in Virginia Beach. They offer two private guest rooms and personalized in-room spa services. Guests are served three-course gourmet breakfasts with personalized service at its best. The inn is eight minutes from Sandbridge Beach and will provide beach chairs, towels, coolers, and umbrellas. There is also an outdoor hot tub and swimming pool.

House and Condo Rentals
There are several local real estate offices in Virginia Beach that offer rentals for a week or longer. **Sandbridge Realty** (800/933-4800, www.sandbridge.com) is in southern Virginia Beach and offers a property search feature on its website, as does **Siebert Realty** (877/422-2200, www.siebert-realty.com), which is also in southern Virginia Beach.

CAMPING
First Landing State Park (2500 Shore Dr., 757/412-2300, www.first-landing-state-park.org, $24-32) on the north end of Virginia Beach offers 200-plus beach campsites near the Chesapeake Bay. There are also 20 cabins for rent ($94-139).

FOOD
American
The **Five 01 City Grill** (501 N. Birdneck, 757/425-7195, www.five01citygrill.com, daily from 5:30pm, $8-26) is a true grill house with an open grill kitchen located right in the dining room. The menu is California fusion-inspired and offers everything from homemade pizza to pasta and seafood and even a little Mexican.

A restaurant popular with Virginia Beach residents is **Rockafeller's** (308 Mediterranean Ave., 757/442-5654, www.rockafellers.com, brunch Sun. 10am-2pm, lunch Mon.-Sat. 11am-3pm, dinner Mon.-Sat. 3pm-10pm, Sun. 2pm-10pm, $11-30). This dependable American favorite offers seafood, steaks, pasta, and salads in a large three-story home on Rudee

Inlet. Double-decker porches provide lovely seating, or you can dine inside. There's a bar and raw bar and nice views from indoors as well.

If you're looking for a good place to grab a sandwich, stop in **Taste Unlimited** (36th Street and Pacific Avenue, 757/422-3399, www.tasteunlimited.com, Mon.-Sat. 10am-6pm, Sun. 11am-5pm, $6-10). This pleasant sandwich shop and specialty food store, a block from the beach, has ample seating, a good variety of choices, and a friendly atmosphere. They also sell wine, cheese, and other gourmet snacks, and at times there's even a little farmer's market outside.

Seafood
◖ **One Fish Two Fish** (2109 W. Great Neck Rd., 757/496-4350, www.onefish-twofish.com, dinner daily from 5pm, $26-34) is an elegant but fun seafood and steak restaurant on Long Creek (in the Pier House building at the Long Bay Pointe Marina). It is comfortably away from the hubbub of the strip, and diners can enjoy a panoramic view of the water or entertain themselves with the exhibition kitchen activity (where guests can watch the chefs at work). There's also an open patio. Seafood combinations are expertly and imaginatively prepared, and they offer an excellent selection of wine.

Catch 31 (3001 Atlantic Ave., 757/213-3474, www.catch31.com, Mon.-Fri. 6am-2am, Sat.-Sun. 7am-2am, $25-43) is inside the Hilton Virginia Beach Oceanfront and is one of the finest restaurants along the main strip. They are known for offering at least 15 types of fresh fish, and their signature dish is the seafood towers that include crab legs, mussels, lobster, and shrimp. Their high ceilings, ocean blue walls, and indoor/outdoor bar add to the ambience. If the weather is nice, dine outside on their beachfront terrace. They serve breakfast, lunch, and dinner.

Lynnhaven Fish House (2350 Starfish Rd., 757/481-0003, www.lynnhavenfishhouse.net, Sun.-Thurs. 11:30am-9pm, Fri.-Sat.

One Fish Two Fish restaurant in Virginia Beach

11:30am-10pm, $15-30) serves up fresh surf dishes with a nice view of the oceanfront. They have a large fish selection on their dinner menu and creative lunch entrées such as seafood omelets and quiche.

The **Waterman's Surfside Grille** (5th Street and Atlantic Avenue, 757/428-3644, www.watermans.com, lunch daily 11am-4pm, dinner daily 4pm-10pm, $15-25) is one of the few freestanding restaurants left on the strip that isn't connected to a hotel. It offers a lively atmosphere, good seafood, and outstanding cocktails.

INFORMATION AND SERVICES

For additional information on Virginia Beach, visit www.virginiabeach.com or stop by the **Visitor Information Center** (2100 Parks Ave., 757/437-4919, daily 9am-5pm). There are also two kiosks run by the Visitor Information Center that are available from May-September located on the Boardwalk at 17th Street and on Atlantic Avenue at 24th Street.

GETTING THERE

Most people arrive in Virginia Beach by car. I-64 connects with the Virginia Beach-Norfolk Expressway (I-264) which leads to the oceanfront at Virginia Beach.

The **Norfolk International Airport** (www.norfolkairport.com, code ORF) is approximately 17 miles from Virginia Beach. Daily flights are available through multiple commercial carriers.

Rail service does not run to Virginia Beach, but **Amtrak** (800/872-7245, www.amtrak.com) offers service to Newport News with connecting bus service to 19th Street and Pacific Avenue. Reservations are required. Bus service is also available to Virginia Beach on **Greyhound** (971 Virginia Beach Blvd., 757/422-2998, www.greyhound.com).

GETTING AROUND

There are plenty of paid parking lots in Virginia Beach. The cost per day ranges about $5-8. Municipal parking lots are located at 4th

Street, 9th Street, 19th Street, 25th Street, and 31st Street. **Hampton Roads Transit** (www. gohrt.com, $1.50-3.50) operates about a dozen bus routes in Virginia Beach.

Virginia's Eastern Shore

Visiting Virginia's Eastern Shore can be a bit like stepping back in time. The long, narrow, flat peninsula that separates the Chesapeake Bay from the Atlantic Ocean has a feel that's very different from the rest of the state. The pace is more relaxed, the people take time to chat, and much of the cuisine centers around extraordinary seafood fished right out the back door.

Traveling from the Virginia Beach area to the Eastern Shore requires passage over and through one of the great marvels of the East Coast. The **Chesapeake Bay Bridge-Tunnel** (www.cbbt.com) spanning the mouth of the Chesapeake Bay is an engineering masterpiece. The four-lane, 20-mile bridge and tunnel system is a toll route and part of Route 13. It takes vehicles over a series of bridges and through two mile-long tunnels that travel under the shipping channels. Five-acre artificial islands are located at each end of the two tunnels, and a fishing pier and restaurant/gift shop were built on one.

Upon arrival on the Eastern Shore, you are greeted by endless acres of marsh, water, and wildlife refuge areas. Agriculture and fishing are the primary sources of revenue on the peninsula, and tourism in the towns provides a nice supplement.

There are a handful of charming towns that dot the coastline on both bodies of water, and most have roots prior to the Civil War. In fact,

© MICHAELA RIVA GAASERUD

Chesapeake Bay Bridge-Tunnel fishing pier

many beautiful 19th-century homes have been refurbished, as have the churches, schools, and public buildings.

The first town on the southern end of the Eastern Shore is Cape Charles, and the northernmost is Chincoteague Island. Bus transportation runs between the two on the **Star Transit** (www.mystartransit.com, Mon.-Fri.).

CAPE CHARLES

Cape Charles is the southernmost town on Virginia's Eastern Shore, 10 miles from the Chesapeake Bay Bridge-Tunnel. The town was founded in 1884 as the southern terminus of the New York, Philadelphia, & Norfolk Railroad. It was also a popular steamship port for vessels transporting freight and passengers across the Chesapeake Bay to Norfolk.

Today, Cape Charles is primarily a vacation town. It is not large, nor is it particularly well known, but this is part of the charm. It offers a quiet historic district, sandy beaches, golfing, boating, and other outdoor recreation.

Sights

The **Historic District** (757/331-3259) in Cape Charles is approximately seven square blocks and boasts one of the largest groups of turn-of-the-20th-century buildings on the East Coast. The historic area offers a pleasant atmosphere of shops and eateries near the Chesapeake Bay waterfront. Route 184 runs right into the historic district and ends at the beach.

Cape Charles Beach (Bay Avenue, www.capecharles.org) provides a pleasant, uncrowded beach atmosphere and wonderful sunsets over the Chesapeake Bay. The beach is clean, family oriented, and free to the public. The water is generally shallow with little to no waves.

The **Cape Charles Museum and Welcome Center** (814 Randolph Ave., 757/331-1008, www.smallmuseum.org, mid-Apr.-Nov. Mon.-Fri. 10am-2pm, Sat. 10am-5pm, Sun. 1pm-5pm, free, donations appreciated) is a nice place to begin your visit to Cape Charles. It is housed in the old Delmarva Power house and has a large generator embedded in the floor. Visitors can view boat models, pictures, and decoys, as they learn about the history of Cape Charles.

The **Kiptopeke State Park** (3540 Kiptopeke Dr., 757/331-2267, www.dcr.virginia.gov, 24 hours, $3) is approximately 10 miles south of the Historic District in Cape Charles. It encompasses a half-mile of sandy beach open to the public during the summer. There are no lifeguards on duty, so swimming is at your own risk. There are also hiking trails, a fishing pier, a boat ramp, and a full-service campground. The park is known for its wonderful bird population. Many bird studies are conducted here by the U.S. Fish and Wildlife Service. Some of the birds encountered in the park include hawks, kestrels, and ospreys.

The **Bay Creek Railway** (www.baycreekrailway.com, Memorial Day-Dec. lunch $30, dinner $60) is a wonderfully restored Interurban train car that offers one-hour dining excursions from Mason Avenue in the Historic District. This, fun, unique dining experience is available for lunch and dinner.

Sports and Recreation

SouthEast Expeditions (239 Mason Ave., 757/331-2680, www.southeastexpeditions.com, starting at $45) offers kayaking tours in Cape Charles. Trips of different lengths are available, and paddlers of all experience levels are welcome.

Golfers will enjoy the beautiful atmosphere and two challenging courses designed by Arnold Palmer and Jack Nicklaus at the **Bay Creek Golf Club** (1 Clubhouse Way, 757/331-8620, www.baycreekgolfclub.com, $70-115).

A big annual event in the Cape Charles area is the **Eastern Shore Birding Festival** (www.esvafestivals.org). The area is one of the most important East Coast migration stops for millions of birds each year, and festivalgoers can observe the spectacle firsthand in early October.

Accommodations
$100-200
The **Fig Street Inn** (711 Tazewell Ave., 757/331-3133, www.figstreetinn.com,

© MICHAELA RIVA GAASERUD

marina at Bay Creek Resort in Cape Charles

$160-200) is a year-round boutique bed-and-breakfast offering four comfortable guest rooms with private bathrooms. Each room has memory foam mattresses, lush towels, flat-screen televisions, wireless Internet, and a jetted tub or gas fireplace. The house has been renovated and is decorated with antiques. The beach and shops are within walking distance.

The **King's Creek Inn** (3018 Bowden Landing, 757/678-6355, www.kingscreekinn.com, $140-210) is a beautiful historic plantation home that has offered guest accommodations since 1746. The home was fully renovated and has four guest rooms with private bathrooms. The inn sits on 2.5 acres and overlooks Kings Creek (with access to the Chesapeake Bay). A private dock is available for guest use. The cozy salon offers a great ambience for breakfast, or guests can enjoy meals on their balconies. The home has a long and exciting history and some interesting legends that include stories of the Underground Railroad and a possible resident ghost.

OVER $300

◀ **Bay Creek Resort** (3335 Stone Rd., 757/331-8742, www.baycreek.net, $350-800) is the premier resort community in Cape Charles. The resort offers rentals of vacation homes, villas, and condos in a well-landscaped waterfront and golf community on more than 1,700 acres. Golf packages are available, and golf condos offer three-bedroom, two-bath units with garages and a balcony or patio. Single-family homes are also available overlooking the golf course. Those who prefer a water view will enjoy the Marina District. Rental options include single-family villas with views of the Chesapeake Bay or the Kings Creek Marina. One- and two-bedroom suites are also available. Nightly and longer-term stays can be accommodated. Visitors can stay in luxurious accommodations or dock their own boat in the large, modern marina. Two delicious restaurants are on the property, one at the marina and the other on the golf course. The staff is extremely helpful and friendly.

Camping

Camping is available at **Kiptopeke State Park** (3540 Kiptopeke Dr., 757/331-2267, www.dcr. virginia.gov). The park has tent sites ($24), rental RVs ($103), a yurt ($92), and a camping lodge (bunkhouse, $47). There is a two-night minimum stay required at the camping lodge during the peak summer season and a seven-night minimum at the yurt and rental RVs. All facilities except the yurt allow pets ($10 fee).

Food

AMERICAN

Aqua (900 Marina Village Circle, 757/331-8660, www.kingscreekmarina.com, Sun.-Thurs. 11:30am-9pm, Fri.-Sat. 11:30am-10pm, closed Mon. Labor Day-Memorial Day, $15-29) is the top choice for food and ambience in Cape Charles. The modern beachfront building houses a trendy, well-stocked bar offering fresh cocktails and local brews. It has lounge and bar seating, and a comfortable waterfront dining room. The food is delicious, with creative seafood menu items, entrées from the land, and extremely fresh salads. The staff is very friendly and knowledgeable about not just the food, but the resort and town itself. The scene is semi-upscale with a lively clientele. This is a great place to bring the family or relax with friends for an unrushed and tasty meal.

Dining for guests and nonguests is available at the **King's Creek Inn** (3018 Bowden Landing, 757/678-6355, www.kingscreekinn. com, Thurs.-Sat. 5pm-10pm, Sun. 1pm-8pm, $14-25). This historic inn offers wonderful, personalized service and delicious homemade meals. Dine by the cozy fire in the Bunbury Bar and Dining Room or on the screened porch in nice weather. A selection of entrées include chicken, filet mignon, crab, and other fish. Gluten-free diets can be accommodated with prior notice.

A Bay Creek Resort Restaurant, the **Coach House Tavern** (1 Clubhouse Way, 757/331-8631, www.baycreekresort.com, Sun.-Thurs. 7am-8pm, Fri.-Sat. 7am-9pm, winter hours: Sun.-Thurs. 8am-8pm, Fri.-Sat. 8am-9pm,

$8-15) is at the golf clubhouse and overlooks the golf course. The rustic ambience of the beautifully appointed building is due in part, to the use of reclaimed wood and bricks from a farmhouse that once stood on the property. The restaurant offers traditional pub fare with exquisite soups and sandwiches. There is patio seating, and the atmosphere all around is upscale and inviting.

For a quick and casual seafood meal, stop in **Sting Ray's Restaurant** (26507 Lankford Hwy., 757/331-1541, www.cape-center.com, daily from 4pm, $5-18). This restaurant shares a roof with a gas station and offers a large variety of seafood and other entrées such as shrimp, clam strips, crab cakes, scallops, pork barbecue, ribs, and pork chops. Order at the counter, and the server will bring the food to your table.

Information

For additional details on Cape Charles, contact the **Northampton County Chamber of Commerce** (757/678-0010, www.ccncchamber.com).

ONANCOCK

Thirty-eight miles north of Cape Charles is the picturesque town of Onancock. Onancock sits on the shore of Onancock Creek and has a deepwater harbor. Cute 19th-century homes with gingerbread trim line the streets, and visitors can shop, visit art galleries, partake in water sports, or just relax and enjoy the tranquil atmosphere. The town was founded back in 1680 by English explorers, but its name is derived from a Native American word "auwannaku," which means, "foggy place."

Onancock was one of 12 original "Royal Ports" under King James in the colonies. Its deepwater access to the Chesapeake Bay made it appealing for ships, and its port provided safety during storms. For more than 250 years, Onancock was the trade center on the Eastern Shore and was closely connected (in terms of commerce) to Norfolk and Baltimore.

The homes along Market Street belonged to sea captains who worked on the Chesapeake Bay. These homes harken back to a time during

© MICHAELA RIVA GAASERUD

Ker Place in Onancock

the steamboat era when Onancock was a stop on the way to trendy Baltimore.

Today, Onancock remains a small working port and offers a pretty port of call for recreational boaters. It has modern boats in its harbor, and outdoor enthusiasts paddle colorful kayaks around its waters. Its wharf is also the jumping-off point for a small ferry that goes to and from Tangier Island. The town is a pleasant place to spend a day or two, and about 1,500 people make it their permanent home. There are free parking areas located around town and by the wharf.

Sights

The key sight in Onancock is **Ker Place** (69 Market St., 757/787-8012, www.virginia.org, Mar.-Dec. Tues.-Sat. 11am-3pm, $5), one of the finest historic federal-style manors on the Eastern Shore. John Shepherd Ker was the owner and a Renaissance man for his time. He was a successful merchant, lawyer, banker, and farmer. His estate was built in 1799 and original sat on 1,500 acres. The home is now

restored to its original appearance and features period antique furniture, detailed plaster work, and rich colors throughout. The headquarters for the **Eastern Shore of Virginia Historical Society** are in the house, and the second floor serves as a museum, the society's library, and archive space. A smaller, newer section of the house serves as a welcome center with a museum shop. Visitors can view Eastern Shore artwork throughout the home and rotating exhibits are displayed regularly. Guided tours are given on the hour, and reservations should be made by calling ahead.

Sports and Recreation

A public boat ramp is located at the wharf and offers a public boat launch for canoes and kayaks ($5 launch fee). **SouthEast Expeditions** (2 King St., 757/354-4386, www.southeastexpeditions.com) offers kayak rentals ($20-45) and tours ($45-125) from the wharf. Guided kayak trips are also offered by two local travel writers and kayak guides through **Burnham Guides LLC** (www.burnhamink.com). Visitors

© MICHAELA RIVA GAASERUD

watercraft rentals in Onancock

arriving by boat can dock at the Town Marina but should call the **Harbor Master** (757/787-7911) for reservations.

Free self-guided walking tours are a fun way to learn about the town. Pick up a tour brochure at the visitor center (located on the wharf) and learn about historic homes and gardens.

Accommodations

The Charlotte Hotel and Restaurant (7 North St., 757/787-7400, www.thecharlotte-hotel.com, $120-150) is a boutique hotel with eight guest rooms. The owners take great pride in this lovely hotel and even made some of the furnishings by hand. There is an award-winning restaurant on-site that can seat more than 30 people, and the American cuisine served is made from local products supplied by watermen and farmers.

The Inn at Onancock (30 North St., 757/787-7711, www.innatonancock.com, $195-215) is a luxurious bed-and-breakfast with five guest rooms, each offering stylish modern bathrooms and feather-top beds. Full-service breakfasts are served in their dining room, or guests can choose to eat on the porch in nice weather. A wine hour is also hosted every evening. Soda and water are available to guests all day.

The **Colonial Manor Inn** (84 Market St., 757/787-2564, www.colonialmanorinn.com, $109-139) offers six spacious rooms decorated with period furnishings. The home was built in 1882 and is the oldest operating inn on the Eastern Shore in Virginia. A delicious full breakfast is served daily.

The Inn & Garden Café (145 Market St., 757/787-8850, www.theinnandgardencafe.com, $110-130) has four guest rooms and was built in 1880. There is a restaurant on-site that can accommodate up to 40 people.

Food

Mallards Restaurant (2 Market St., 757/787-8558, www.mallardsllc.com, lunch Tues.-Sat. 11:30am-4pm, Sun.-Mon. 11:30am-9pm, dinner Tues.-Thurs. 5pm-9pm, Fri.-Sat.

5pm-10pm, $8-25) is on the wharf. The menu includes fresh seafood, ribs, duck, pasta, and many more delicious entrées. Don't be surprised if chef Johnny Mo comes out of the kitchen with his guitar to play a few tunes. He's a local legend.

The **Blarney Stone Pub** (10 North St., 757/302-0300, www.blarneystonepubonancock.com, Tues.-Fri. 11am-9pm, Sat. noon-9pm, $8-24) is an Irish pub three blocks from the wharf serving traditional pub fare. It has indoor and outdoor seating and also frequently live entertainment.

If you're making the drive between Onancock and Cape Charles and need a sugary snack, drive through Exmore on Business 13 and stop at the **Yellow Duck Bakery** (3312 Main St., Exmore, 757/442-5909, www.yellowduckcafe.com, Mon.-Wed. 7am-3pm, Thurs.-Fri. 7am-5pm, Sat. 8am-3pm, under $10). They offer amazing sweet potato biscuits, shortbread "Yellow Duck" cookies, other types of cookies, and delicious muffins. You can drive through town and pick up Route 13 again on the other side.

Information and Services

Additional information on Onancock can be found at www.onancock.org. There is also a small, seasonal visitor center at the wharf.

◖ TANGIER ISLAND

Tangier Island is a small 3.5-mile-long island, 12 miles off the coast of Virginia in the middle of the Chesapeake Bay. It was first named as part of a group of small islands called the Russell Isles in 1608 by Captain John Smith when he sailed upon it during an exploration trip of the Chesapeake Bay. At the time the island was the fishing and hunting area of the Pocomoke Indians, but it was allegedly purchased from them in 1666 for the sum of two overcoats. Settlers were drawn to the island for the abundant oyster and crab fishing.

The unofficial history of the island states that John Crockett first settled here with his eight sons in 1686. This appears to be accurate since most of the 600 people who live on Tangier Island today are descendants of the Crockett family and the majority of the tombstones on the island bear the Crockett name. The island was occupied by British troops during the Revolutionary War, and it has also survived four major epidemics, with the most devastating being the Asian cholera epidemic of 1866. So many people died in such a short period of time that family members buried their dead in their front yards. Cement crypts can still be seen in many yards on the island.

There is a tiny airstrip, used primarily for the transport of supplies, but most visitors come by ferry (without their cars). There are no true roads on the island and golf carts and bicycles are used to get around.

Tangier Island is only five feet above sea level, and it is known as the "soft-shell crab capital" for its delectable local crabs. It is also known for the unique dialect the people on Tangier Island speak. They converse in an old form of English and have many euphemisms that are unfamiliar to visitors. It is thought that the island's isolation played a role in preserving the language that was spoken throughout the Tidewater area generations ago.

Tangier Island can be toured in a couple of hours. The ferry schedules are such that they allow enough time to cover the sights on the island, grab lunch, and head back the same day. If you enjoy the slow pace of the island, limited overnight accommodations are available, but be aware there is not much, if any, nightlife and the island is "dry." Addresses aren't frequently used when describing how to get to a place on Tangier Island. Basically, you can see the whole island from any given point. The ferry dock drops visitors off in the heart of the small commercial area, and if you can't see the establishment you are looking for immediately, take a short walk or ride down the main path and you'll find it. The island residents are also very friendly, so if in doubt, just ask someone walking by.

There are very limited services on Tangier Island. The island hasn't changed much in the last century, and it looks much as it did 30 or 40 years ago. There is a post office and one

© MICHAELA RIVA GAASERUD

harbor at Tangier Island

school where all local children attend (most go on to college elsewhere in the state). There is spotty cell service on the island, but some establishments do offer wireless Internet. More important, there are no emergency medical facilities on the island; however, there is a 24-hour clinic, **The Tangier Island Health Foundation** (tangierclinic.org), where a physician's assistant is available.

Many establishments do not accept credit cards, so it's best to bring cash and checks. There are no banks or ATMs on the island.

Sights
TANGIER HISTORY MUSEUM AND INTERPRETIVE CENTER
The **Tangier History Museum and Interpretive Center** (16215 Main Ridge, 757/891-2374, www.tangierhistorymuseum. org, mid-May-mid-Oct. daily 11am-4pm, other times by appointment, $3) is a small museum down the street from the ferry dock. It is worth a visit and the small fee to learn about life on Tangier Island and its interesting heritage.

View island artifacts and a rare five-layered painting of the island that illustrates the erosion it has experienced since 1866. Visitors can also learn about the many sayings that are common on the island but completely foreign to those on the mainland such as "He's adrift," which means, "He's a hunk," and the term "snapjack" which means "firecracker." A handful of kayaks are available behind the museum for visitors to borrow (for free) for exploring the surrounding waterways.

TANGIER BEACH
At the south end of Tangier Island is the nice, sandy public **Tangier Beach.** Rent a golf cart from **Four Brothers** and head out of the village on the winding paved path and over the canal bridge. The beach is at the very end of the path on the left side of the island. There's a small parking area for carts and a sandy path to the beach. There is no lifeguard on duty so swimming is at your own risk. Bring plenty of water with you since there are also no services at the beach. Water machines and soda machines can

be found along the golf cart paths on the island if you need to pick up beverages on your way. There is also a very small grocery store near the ferry dock with a few bare essentials, but it's best to bring provisions with you.

Shopping

There are two small gift shops on Tangier Island: **Wanda's Gifts** (757/891-2230) and **Sandy's Gifts** (757/891-2367). Both are on the main path not far from the ferry dock. They sell souvenir T-shirts and trinkets.

Sports and Recreation

Kayaking through the waterways of Tangier Island is a wonderful way to explore the marshes. Kayaks can be borrowed from the Tangier History Museum, and a listing of water trail routes can be found at www.tangierisland-va.com. The marshes also offer a terrific opportunity for bird-watching. Black skimmers, great blue herons, common terns, double-crested cormorants, Forster's terns, clapper rails, and ospreys are just some of the birds living on the island.

Since there are no roads on Tangier—only paved paths—the place is very conducive to casual biking. Bikes can be brought over on the ferry on weekdays only (call ahead to schedule) and a fleet of older model cruising bikes can be rented from **Four Brothers** (www.fourbrotherscrabhouse.com) on the island. Since the island is only 3.5 miles long, it is easy to cover the entire length by bicycle in a short time.

For a unique local's experience, take a **Crab Shanty Tour** (757/891-2269, ask for Ookire). This half hour to 45-minute tour led by a Chesapeake Bay waterman is a truly unique experience. Other island tours are available outside the ferry dock. Tour guides wait in golf carts for guests when the ferries arrive and offer guided tours in their vehicles.

Accommodations

It is difficult to find more friendly innkeepers than those at the **Bay View Inn** (757/891-2396, www.tangierisland-va.com, $120-150). This family-run bed-and-breakfast offers seven motel-style rooms, two cottages, and two guest rooms in the main house. A lovely homemade breakfast is included with your stay. The inn is on the west side of the island and has lovely views of the Chesapeake Bay and decks to watch the sunset from. The inn is open year-round. They do not take credit cards.

The **Hilda Crockett's Chesapeake House** (757/891-2331, www.tangierisland-va.com, $100-145) is the oldest operating bed-and-breakfast on the island and was established in 1939 as a boardinghouse. It is in the small commercial area not far from the ferry dock. There are eight guest rooms in two separate buildings.

Those arriving by private boat can rent a slip at the **James Parks Marina** (16070 Parks Marina Ln., 757/891-2581). They offer 25 slips and showers, but no pump outs. Docking fees start at $25.

Food

Visitors arriving by ferry will likely see the **Waterfront** (757/891-2248, mid-May-Nov. 1 Mon.-Sat. 10am-4pm, Sun. 1pm-4pm, under $15) as they depart the ferry. This small, seasonal restaurant is right by the dock and offers a variety of casual food including burgers, fried seafood baskets, and crab cakes. **Four Brothers Crab House & Ice Cream Deck** (757/891-2999, www.fourbrotherscrabhouse.com, lunch and dinner daily) will likely be the next establishment you see when you take the short path from the dock to the main path in the small commercial area. While this is the place to rent golf carts, crabbing equipment, and bicycles, they also serve a casual menu of seafood and sandwiches on their deck and 60 soft serve ice cream flavors. Four Brothers also offers free wireless Internet, however, they do not accept credit cards. Another fun place for ice cream is **Spanky's Place** just down the path.

A short walk from the ferry terminal is **Lorraine's Restaurant** (757/891-2225, lunch Mon.-Sat. 10am-2pm, dinner Mon.-Fri. 5pm-10pm, Sat. 5pm-11pm, Sun. noon-5pm, under $15). Take a right on Main Street, and the restaurant is on the right. They serve snacks, lunch, and dinner. Like all the restaurants on

© MICHAELA RIVA GAASERUD

ferry to Tangier Island

the island, local, fresh seafood is the specialty, and this place is known for the soft shell crabs. Lorraine's also delivers to any of the inns on the island.

Across from Lorraine's, **Fisherman's Corner Restaurant** (757/891-2900, www.fishermanscornerrestaurant.com, daily 11am-7pm, $10-20) has a wide menu with steaks and seafood. Sandwiches and a kid's menu are also available. It's no surprise that fresh crab is a special feature, and their crab cakes contain large succulent blue crab meat with little filler.

The best-known and oldest restaurant on the island is ◖ **Hilda Crockett's Chesapeake House** (757/891-2331, breakfast daily 7am-9am, lunch/dinner daily 11:30am-5pm, breakfast $9, lunch/dinner $22). They offer an all-you-can-eat breakfast with selections such as scrambled eggs, fried bread, and potatoes. They are most famous, however, for the family-style lunch and dinner. For $22, guests can enjoy unlimited homemade crab cakes, clam fritters, ham, potato salad, coleslaw, pickled beets, applesauce, green beans, corn pudding, and rolls.

The family-style setting means you may share a table with other guests.

Information and Services

For additional information, visit www.tangier-island.com.

Getting There

Getting to Tangier Island is half the fun. There are three seasonal ferries that travel to and from the island May-October. The first is the *Chesapeake Breeze* (804/453-2628, www.tangiercruise.com, $27 round-trip for same-day service, $40 for overnight), a 150-person passenger boat, which leaves at 10am daily from Reedville for the 1.5-hour trip. The ship heads back to Reedville at 2:15pm. The second is the *Steven Thomas* (800/863-2338, www.tangierislandcruises.com, $27 round-trip for same-day service, $35 for overnight), a 90-foot, 300-passenger boat, that leaves from Crisfield, Maryland, daily (May 15-Oct. 15) at 12:30pm and arrives on Tangier at 1:45pm. The return voyage departs Tangier at 4pm. The third ferry is the *Joyce Marie II* (757/891-2505, www.tangierferry.com, $25 round-trip for same-day service, $30 for overnight), a small fiberglass lobster boat that holds 25 people and runs from Onancock, Virginia, to Tangier Island. The trip takes an hour and five minutes. Ferry service is offered twice a day with departures from Tangier Island at 7:30am and 3:30pm and departures from Onancock at 10am and 5pm.

Getting Around
There are no cars on Tangier Island. The best way to get around is by renting a golf cart from **Four Brothers Crab House & Ice Cream Deck** ($50 for 24 hours, $25 for a half day) or a bicycle ($10 a day). The owners will make you feel welcome immediately, and Tommy is sure to put you in a good mood for your ride around town when he turns over the keys to your cart.

CHINCOTEAGUE ISLAND
Chincoteague Island is 7 miles long and just 1.5 miles wide. It is nestled between the Eastern Shore and Assateague Island. Chincoteague is famous for its herd of wild ponies, and many children and adults first became familiar with the island through the popular book, *Misty of Chincoteague,* which was published in 1947. Many local residents made appearances in the movie that followed.

The island is in the far northeastern region of the Eastern Shore in Virginia and has a full-time population of 4,300 residents. It attracts more than one million visitors each year to enjoy the pretty town and to visit the Chincoteague National Wildlife Refuge and the beautiful nearby beach on Assateague Island.

Chincoteague is a working fishing village with world-famous oyster beds and clam shoals. It is also a popular destination for bird-watching. During the summer, the town is bustling with tourists, but in the off-season things slow down considerably and many establishments close.

The town of Chincoteague is accessed via Route 175. A long scenic causeway crosses over water and marsh and ends on Main Street, which runs along the western shore of the island. Maddox Boulevard meets Main Street and runs east to the visitor center and Chincoteague National Wildlife Refuge.

Sights
◖ CHINCOTEAGUE NATIONAL WILDLIFE REFUGE
The **Chincoteague National Wildlife Refuge** (8231 Beach Rd., 757/336-6122, www.fws.gov, May-Sept. daily 5am-10pm, Mar.-Apr. and Oct. daily 6am-8pm, Nov.-Feb. daily 6am-6pm, $8) is a 14,000-acre refuge consisting of beach, dunes, marsh, and maritime forest on the Virginia end of Assateague Island and was established in 1943. The area is a thriving habitat for many species of waterfowl, shorebirds, songbirds, and wading birds. The popular herd of wild ponies that Chincoteague is known for also lives in the refuge.

Assateague Island itself, extends south from Ocean City, Maryland, to just south of Chincoteague Island. It is a thin strip of beautiful sand beach, approximately 37 miles long. The entire beach is a National Seashore, and the Virginia side is where the Chincoteague National Wildlife Refuge is located. The refuge entrance is at the end of Maddox Boulevard. A visitor center is situated near the beach where information and trail brochures can be obtained. One of the main attractions is the **Assateague Island Lighthouse,** which visitors can hike to. The lighthouse is painted with red and white stripes and is 142 feet tall. It was completed in 1867 and is still operational. There are also 15 miles of woodland trails for hiking and biking (the wild ponies can often be seen from the trails).

The road ends at the Atlantic Ocean where there's a large parking area for beachgoers. Parts of the beach are open to swimming, surfing, clamming, and crabbing.

To get to the refuge, travel east on Route 175 onto Chincoteague Island and continue straight at the traffic light onto Maddox Boulevard. Follow the signs to the refuge.

OYSTER AND MARITIME MUSEUM

The only oyster museum in the country is in Chincoteague. The **Oyster and Maritime Museum** (7125 Maddox Blvd., 757/336-6117, Tues.-Sun. 11am-5pm, $3) is on Maddox Boulevard just prior to the entrance to the National Wildlife Refuge. The museum is dedicated to sharing the history of the island and details of the oyster trade and the local seafood industry. One of the most noteworthy exhibits in the museum is the Fresnel lens that was part of the Assateague Island Lighthouse. This lens helped guide ships as far out to sea as 23 miles for nearly 96 years.

CHINCOTEAGUE PONY CENTRE

For those wishing to see the local ponies up close, the **Chincoteague Pony Centre** (6417 Carriage Dr., 757/336-2776, www.chincoteague.com/ponycentre, Mon.-Sat. during summer) has a herd of ponies from the island in their stable and a field facility for visitors to enjoy. The center offers pony rides, riding lessons, shows, day camps, and a large gift shop.

Entertainment and Events

The premier event on Chincoteague Island is the annual **Wild Pony Swim** (www.chincoteaguechamber.com) that takes place each year in late July. At "slack tide," usually in the morning, the herd of wild ponies is made to swim across the Assateague Channel on the east side of Chincoteague Island (those ponies that are not strong enough or are too small to make the swim are ferried across on barges). The first foal to complete the swim is named "King" or "Queen" Neptune and is given away in a raffle later that day. After the swim, the ponies are given a short rest and are then paraded to the carnival grounds on Main Street. The annual Pony Penning and Auction is then held where some foals and yearlings are auctioned off. Benefits from the auction go to support the local fire and ambulance services. The remaining herd then swims back across the channel.

© MICHAELA RIVA GAASERUD

Chincoteague Pony Centre on Chincoteague Island

Another big event in town is the **Chincoteague Island Oyster Festival** (8128 Beebe Rd., www.chincoteagueoysterfestival. com, $40). This well-known event has been happening for more than 40 years and offers all you can eat oysters prepared every which way imaginable. It is held in early October, and tickets are available online.

Sports and Recreation

Kayaks can be launched on the beach on Assateague Island, but not in areas patrolled by lifeguards. Kayak rentals are available through **Assateague Explorer** (www.assateagueexplorer.com, single half day $39, full day $49, tandem half day $55, full day $65). They also offer kayak tours and pony-viewing tours that launch from their private dock ($45-55). **Snug Harbor Resort** (7536 East Side Rd., 757/336-6176, www.chincoteagueaccommodations.com, single half day $38, full day $48, tandem half day $48, full day $58) also rents kayaks, canoes, and other personal watercraft.

Jus' Bikes (6527 Maddox Blvd., 757/336-6700, www.jus-bikes.com) rents bicycles ($4 per hour or $12 per day), scooters ($15 per hour or $50 per day), surreys ($20 per hour or $75 per day), tandems ($5 per hour or $25 per day), three-wheelers ($3 per hour or $18 per day), and Scoot Coupes Cars ($35 per hour or $150 per day).

Fishing enthusiasts can have all their needs met at several fishing and tackle establishments including **Barnacle Bill's Bait & Tackle** (3691 Main St., 757/336-5920), **Capt Bob's Marina** (2477 Main St., 757/336-6654), and **Capt Steves Bait & Tackle** (6527 Maddox Blvd., 757/336-0569).

For an interactive cruise, contact **Captain Barry's Back Bay Cruises** (6262 Main St., 757/336-6508, www.captainbarry. net). They offer hands-on, interactive "Sea Life Expeditions" ($35) and "Champagne Sunset Cruises" ($40) leaving from the Chincoteague Inn Restaurant at 6262 Main Street.

Accommodations

$100-200

If you're looking for a charming bed-and-breakfast, spend a night at **❮ Miss Molly's Inn** (4141 Main St., 757/336-6686, www.missmollys-inn.com, $110-200) on Main Street. This beautiful Victorian B&B offers seven delightful guest rooms and five porches with rocking chairs. The home overlooks the bay and has a pretty English garden. Marguerite Henry stayed at the bed-and-breakfast when she wrote the famous book *Misty of Chincoteague,* and the room she stayed in has since been named after her. A full breakfast is included. The sister inn to Miss Molly's is the **Island Manor House Bed and Breakfast** (4160 Main St., 757/336-5436, www.island-manor.com, $165-210), which offers eight guest rooms and plenty of common areas. This house was built in the popular Maryland T style, which borrows from both federal and Georgian architecture. Refreshments are available 24 hours a day. They provide a gourmet breakfast each day and easy access to Main Street attractions.

The **Dove Winds** (7023 Maddox Blvd., 757/336-5667, www.dovewinds.com, $85-150) is a nice, clean hotel offering mini townhouses for rent with two-bedroom guest accommodations. The units aren't fancy, but they are comfortable and offer more privacy than a typical hotel. Each includes a kitchen, living room, and two bathrooms. They also offer two- and three-bedroom cottages. An indoor pool and hot tub are on-site.

$200-300

The **❮ Hampton Inn & Suites Chincoteague Waterfront** (4179 Main St., 757/336-1616, www.hamptoninnchincoteague.com, $229-289) is known as one of the premier Hampton Inns in the country. Its bay-front location offers beautiful views, and it is close to many shops and restaurants in town. The rooms are well appointed with light wood furniture, and everything is oriented toward the water. The landscaping is appealing, the breakfasts are better than standard chain fare, and there is a boat dock next to the hotel. Amenities include a large indoor heated pool, a fitness center, laundry facilities, a waterfront veranda, and wireless Internet. The staff and owner are also very friendly. Ask for a room on the third floor with a balcony looking over the water.

Camping

Camping is available on Chincoteague Island at several campgrounds. The **Maddox Family Campground** (6742 Maddox Blvd., 757/336-3111, www.chincoteague.com, $40) offer 550 campsites and 361 utility hookups March-November. **Tom's Cove Campground** (8128 Beebe Rd., 757/336-6498, www.tomscove-park.com, $32-52) offers waterfront campsites near the pony swim, three fishing piers, and a pool. They are open March-November. **Pine Grove Campground** (5283 Deep Hole Rd., 757/336-5200, www.pinegrovecampground.com, $33-43) offers campsites on 37 acres April-November. There are six ponds on-site.

Food
AMERICAN

If you like a casual beach environment, eating outside, and lounging in hammocks, then **Woody's Beach Barbeque and Eatery** (6700 Maddox Blvd., www.woodysbeachbbq.com, Mon.-Sat. 11am-8pm, Sun. 1pm-8pm, $6-20) is worth checking out. They offer delightful barbecue and crab sandwiches, yummy sweet potato fries, and peach tea. There are also outdoor games for the kids.

For a quick bite to go, stop at the ◖ **Sea Star Café** (6429 Maddox Blvd., 757/336-5442, Thurs.-Mon. 11am-6pm, $5-10). They offer yummy sandwiches and wraps to go (order at the window and be ready when there's a crowd). Everything is fresh and made to order, and they have a large vegetarian menu. The café sits back off the road a little and offers a few picnic tables but no restrooms. The menu is handwritten on a chalkboard and items contain whatever is fresh that day.

SEAFOOD

Seafood is the mainstay on Chincoteague Island, and the local oysters and crabs are especially delicious. Many restaurants are only open seasonally; so visiting in the off-season can pose a bit of a challenge in finding open eateries.

AJ's on the Creek (6585 Maddox Blvd., 757/336-5888, www.ajsonthecreek.com, Mar.-Dec. Mon.-Thurs. 11:30am-8:30pm, Fri.-Sat. 11:30am-9:30pm, $18-30) is the longest operating restaurant on the island under one management. They are one of a few upscale restaurants on the island, and they serve delicious seafood menu items such as crab imperial, shellfish bouillabaisse, crab cakes, and grilled scallops. The restaurant is owned by two spunky sisters originally from Pittsburgh.

Don't let the plain exterior of **Bill's Seafood Restaurant** (4040 Main St., 757/336-5831, www.billsseafoodrestaurant.com, daily from 6am for breakfast, lunch, and dinner, $12-27) fool you. They offer delightful seafood entrées such as lobster tail, scallops, oysters, and crab cakes, as well as pasta selections. This is one of the few restaurants in town that is open all year.

TREATS

The **Island Creamery** (6243 Maddox Blvd., 757/336-6236, www.islandcreamery.net, year-round daily 11am-10pm) is "the" place to go for ice cream. The place is large for an ice cream joint and offers friendly smiles, samples, and dozens of flavors. It's a popular stop, so the line can be long and parking difficult, but it's worth it.

Information and Services

For additional information on Chincoteague Island, visit www.chincoteaguechamber.com or stop by the **Chincoteague Island Visitor's Center** (6733 Maddox Blvd., 757/336-6161, Mon.-Sat. 9am-4:30pm).

Getting There

Visitors must arrive on Chincoteague Island by car. The closest airport is **Wicomico Regional Airport** (410/548-4827), which is 52 miles away in Salisbury, Maryland.

MAP SYMBOLS

▨▨▨	Expressway	◧	Highlight	✗	Airfield	⌁	Golf Course
▨▨▨	Primary Road	○	City/Town	✗	Airport	▣	Parking Area
▨▨▨	Secondary Road	◉	State Capital	▲	Mountain	▟	Archaeological Site
- - - -	Unpaved Road	⊛	National Capital	+	Unique Natural Feature	▮	Church
- - - - -	Trail	★	Point of Interest			▮	Gas Station
··········	Ferry	•	Accommodation	🗺	Waterfall	〰	Glacier
- - - - -	Railroad	▼	Restaurant/Bar	▲	Park	◿	Mangrove
▨▨▨	Pedestrian Walkway	▪	Other Location	◨	Trailhead	▨	Reef
▨▨▨	Stairs	∆	Campground	✗	Skiing Area	▨	Swamp

CONVERSION TABLES

$°C = (°F - 32) / 1.8$
$°F = (°C \times 1.8) + 32$
1 inch = 2.54 centimeters (cm)
1 foot = 0.304 meters (m)
1 yard = 0.914 meters
1 mile = 1.6093 kilometers (km)
1 km = 0.6214 miles
1 fathom = 1.8288 m
1 chain = 20.1168 m
1 furlong = 201.168 m
1 acre = 0.4047 hectares
1 sq km = 100 hectares
1 sq mile = 2.59 square km
1 ounce = 28.35 grams
1 pound = 0.4536 kilograms
1 short ton = 0.90718 metric ton
1 short ton = 2,000 pounds
1 long ton = 1.016 metric tons
1 long ton = 2,240 pounds
1 metric ton = 1,000 kilograms
1 quart = 0.94635 liters
1 US gallon = 3.7854 liters
1 Imperial gallon = 4.5459 liters
1 nautical mile = 1.852 km

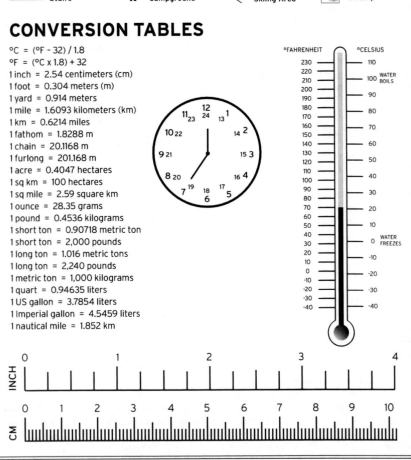

MOON COASTAL VIRGINIA
Avalon Travel
a member of the Perseus Books Group
1700 Fourth Street
Berkeley, CA 94710, USA
www.moon.com

Editor and Series Manager: Kathryn Ettinger
Copy Editor: Ashley Benning
Graphics Coordinator: Elizabeth Jang
Production Coordinator: Elizabeth Jang
Cover Designer: Kathryn Osgood
Map Editor: Mike Morgenfeld
Cartographers: Brian Shotwell, Stephanie Poulain

ISBN-13: 978-1-61238-782-6

Text © 2014 by Michaela Riva Gaaserud.
Maps © 2014 by Avalon Travel.
All rights reserved.

KEEPING CURRENT

If you have a favorite gem you'd like to see included in the next edition, or see anything that needs updating, clarification, or correction, please drop us a line. Send your comments via email to feedback@moon.com, or use the address above.

ABOUT THE AUTHOR

Michaela Riva Gaaserud

Michaela Riva Gaaserud is a native Virginian and longtime resident of the Washington DC area. Some of her earliest memories are of playing travel guide to visiting relatives as they went to the museums and monuments in Washington DC. Inspired by the enthusiasm she witnessed from first-timers to the city, Michaela began looking for hidden secrets to share with her audience. A particularly inspiring school field trip to the underground depths of the Lincoln Memorial sealed her love for discovering and sharing the marvels of her own backyard.

Michaela has published travel guides on various aspects of the Washington DC region. Her articles have appeared in newspapers, magazines, and international publications such as *Canoe & Kayak Magazine* and *Paddler Magazine*. Other publications include *Lake Placid: With the Olympic Village, Lake George and New York's Adirondacks; From Fairbanks to Boston: 50 Great U.S. Marathons; From Kona to Lake Placid: 50 Great U.S. Triathlons;* and *Sea Kayaking the Baltimore/Washington, D.C. Area.* After the publication of this last book, she became a sought-after speaker and was featured in a kayaking documentary. She is also a founding partner at Rainmaker Publishing and an executive producer at Eddyline Media.

CPSIA information can be obtained at www.ICGtesting.com
Printed in the USA
LVOW12n1218030614

388390LV00001B/1/P